Sung-Jo Park

Megatrend University in Serbia

AF720824

Global Cultural and Economic Research

editors-in-chief:

Prof. em. Dr. Dr. h.c. Sung-Jo Park
(Free University Berlin)

and

Prof. Dr. Mica Jovanovic
(Megatrend University
of Applied Sciences, Belgrade)

Volume 9

LIT

Sung-Jo Park

Megatrend University in Serbia

A Model Case of Capacity Building in System Transformation

LIT

Gedruckt auf alterungsbeständigem Werkdruckpapier entsprechend
ANSI Z3948 DIN ISO 9706

Bibliographic information published by the Deutsche Nationalbibliothek
The Deutsche Nationalbibliothek lists this publication in the Deutsche Nationalbibliografie; detailed bibliographic data are available in the Internet at http://dnb.d-nb.de.

ISBN 978-3-643-90214-6

A catalogue record for this book is available from the British Library

©LIT VERLAG GmbH & Co. KG Wien,
Zweigniederlassung Zürich 2013
Klosbachstr. 107
CH-8032 Zürich
Tel. +41 (0) 44-251 75 05
Fax +41 (0) 44-251 75 06
E-Mail: zuerich@lit-verlag.ch
http://www.lit-verlag.ch

LIT VERLAG Dr. W. Hopf
Berlin 2013
Fresnostr. 2
D-48159 Münster
Tel. +49 (0) 2 51-62 03 20
Fax +49 (0) 2 51-23 19 72
E-Mail: lit@lit-verlag.de
http://www.lit-verlag.de

Distribution:
In Germany: LIT Verlag Fresnostr. 2, D-48159 Münster
Tel. +49 (0) 2 51-620 32 22, Fax +49 (0) 2 51-922 60 99, E-mail: vertrieb@lit-verlag.de
In Austria: Medienlogistik Pichler-ÖBZ, e-mail: mlo@medien-logistik.at
In Switzerland: B + M Buch- und Medienvertrieb, e-mail: order@buch-medien.ch
In the UK: Global Book Marketing, e-mail: mo@centralbooks.com
In North America: International Specialized Book Services, e-mail: orders@isbs.com

This book is dedicated to Mića.

Belgrade, 27/12/99

„The new forms of education and training of the professional staff are considered as strategic goals in the development process of the so-called „participation of the organization" which should respond to numerous needs and aspirations of the nations of different origins and cultures, but live together in Europe.
The old Europe is moving towards The New Europe based on cultural regions, thus creating new mechanisms of external relations and internal cohesion.
'The New Europe will depend on the success of transnational and transcultural interaction of knowledge and cultures'."

(Cited from the Website of Megatrend University)

The author
Prof. em. Dr. Dr. h.c. **Sung-Jo Park**
Free University Berlin
Former President of Megatrend University,
President of Euro Asia Management Studies Association
and Secretary General of Global University Network

Table of Contents

1. Instead of Preface

Introductory Remarks by Renowned Scholars about Megatrend University

This book is conceptualized as an anthology of essays and stories related to Megatrend University. It begins with the testimony of impressions that Megatrend University made on prominent visitors.

Dr. Galen Amstutz, then working at Harvard University, was invited to give lectures at Megatrend University during his visiting professorship in 2002 at Free University Berlin. He gave his impression on Megatrend University in the following summary.

Mića Jovanović and Galen Amstutz 2002 in Belgrade

"I was invited to Megatrend in April 2002 from Harvard University's Reischauer Institute as a special lecturer. At the time, Megatrend appeared to be getting established in the post-Communist environment in a set of urban buildings. I spoke on problems of consumer capitalism to a large, enthusiastic audience of students who seemed to handle the English-language lecture well, and who were probably just as familiar with the arguments as I. Professor and President Jovanović was extremely hospitable and energetic... My impression was of an ambitious private university moving forward successfully in an entirely new market environment. These observations were most educational for me because the market in the USA is already relatively organized and few USA presidents face the kind of challenges posed to Jovanović." (16. Jan.2011)

***Prof. Arthur Stockwin* (Oxford University) visited Megatrend University in 2002 in order to deliver special lectures. In the following, he stated his impression on Megatrend University.**

"In March 2002, I enjoyed the fascinating experience of lecturing on the politics of Japan to students at Megatrend University, Belgrade. My visit was arranged through the good offices of my friend, Professor Park, Sung Jo, of the Free University of Berlin. At that time, the University was some 12 years old and the terrible wars that had broken Yugoslavia apart were a painfully recent memory. It had been founded by the larger-than-life figure of Professor Mića Jovanović, just as Eastern Europe was emerging from the Cold War, and by the time I visited it was already the largest private tertiary educational institution in South-eastern Europe.

The entrepreneurial spirit of Professor Jovanović was evident in dynamism of this still young university, and in the enthusiasm of the members of its staff that I met. When I was there it was still at that experimental phase that new institutions go through, where various futures seem possible, and procedures have not yet firmed up into bureaucratic rigidity. The number of enrolled students had expanded rapidly and had already reached around 8,000. Among the courses offered there was a strong emphasis on business and management studies, which were seen as appropriate to a local economy still recovering from war and needing to recruit a pool of highly educated entrepreneurial talent. Based on a perceptive understanding of globalising trends in the world economy, the concept of 'inter-cultural management' was a term I heard widely used during my visit.

Arthur Stockwin during his lecture in 2002 at Megatrend

I left Belgrade at the end of my visit with a strong impression of a people recently traumatised by war, but now determined to create a sane and progressive economy and society. At Megatrend University, what I saw could be described as the flowering of a creative spirit. Clearly many difficulties lay ahead, but the determination to surmount these through enterprise and hard work was clear.

I would like to congratulate Megatrend University, and its founder, Professor Mića Jovanović, on reaching the twentieth anniversary of this wonderful institution." (28. Jan. 2011)

***Prof. Tetsuo Abo*, (Emeritus of University of Tokyo), gave special lectures on his very famous "hybrid factory" theory during his visit to Megatrend University in 1989. He sent the author the following impression on Megatrend University.**

"In my uncertain memory it was the initial or even preparing time (in 1989) for Megatrend University that I and a couple of other British and Japanese researchers (Dr. Stephen Wood (LSE), Prof. Shoichiro Sei (Kanto Gakuin University) and so on) gave lectures on management and economies at some big room of a university (Univ. of Belgrade). We were invited by Prof. Mića Jovanović (Univ. of Belgrade), introduced by Prof. S-J. Park (Free Univ. of Berlin).

Professor Tetsuo Abo

I gave lectures on Japanese management and its international transfer. Frankly speaking, at first I was in doubt how it could be useful for students in such a developing country to learn management or business matters. However, students or audience, a mixture of young and old, and mostly working people from various work places, were very eager to absorb new knowledge and technologies needed for up grading the level of their industries as a newly developing country at that time. The auto company Yugo America (Zastava) started to sell its small and cheapest cars in the USA in 1985. But lots of mechanical problems followed on and in 1989 the company went bankrupt. And on the way of its revival activities in the early 1990's Yugoslavia was in the unhappy war. Nevertheless, Prof. Jovanović's far-reaching plan to build up the Megatrend University has vigorously survived since then

I enjoyed walking around the beautiful old streets of Belgrade with other guests. I bought several nice souvenirs and I still wear one of them with love, a well-designed green cotton shirt. I have been wondering whether those streets managed to endure the war." (March 11, 2011)

They who know the truth are not equal to those who love it,
and they who love it are not equal to those who delight in it.

(Confucius)

Private business schools in former socialist economies are mushrooming. *One group* of these schools is being established by means of *differentiated* and *gradual* introduction of Western management education contents and methods (*gradualism*).

The *other group* is enthusiastic to introduce Western management principles and techniques in a very rapid manner in order to reach success within a short period which is known as *crash therapy.*

The author of this book prefers gradualism approach beginning with capacity-building *'comprising the abilities of individuals, communities, institutions, organizations and political systems to make use of natural, political, social and human resources… available'.(UNDP's definition)*

Those favoring gradual efforts to build up a sustainable basis for human resources development in a longer time period called 'gradualists' stress, first of all, a change of socialism-socialized personalities, whilst others, the so-called *'crash-transformationists'* place on a radical change of socialist economy legacies. Most of crash-therapy experts think that it is possible to introduce market economy *before* market actors and institutional frameworks are created or begin to function to a certain degree. For the supporters of crash therapy, it is argued that there is *no alternative* but to abolish legacies of socialist economy and to set up a new market economy.

Here we have one of the most successful gradualism cases in system transformation which has begun with capacity-building.

Megatrend University

It was founded in 1989 as the first private university in Southeast Europe, now with

- 26.000 students,
- 615 Professors,
- more than 20 international partnerships
- 8 local detachments, and
- 4 foreign dependences (London, Paris, Tokyo, Vienna).

It became the most successful higher education institution in South-east Europe with an excellent recognition by EU, and national as well as international higher education-institutions. This university is regionally and globally networked, known for actively pursuing student and faculty exchange, hosting regional and global seminars, and being awarded for making contribution to local development.

The author has accompanied the project Megatrend University from the stage of conceptualization, planning and practical implementation in terms of executive trainings which were carried out before the foundation of the university. He feels privileged to extensively describe (unknown) stories and histories related to birth and development of this university. The intention of the author is also to present a model case of successful transformation in capacity-building.

At this place the author should not forget to name scholars and experts worldwide to feel solidarity with this university.

- Abo Tetsuo, formerly University of Tokyo,
- Nomura Masami, Tohoku University,
- Kim Byungsub, Seoul National University,
- Rebecca Morales, formerly UCLA,
- Galen Amstutz, formerly Harvard University,
- Arthur Stockwin, Oxford University,
- Andras Hernadi, Hungarian Academy of Sciences,
- Sam Dzever, formerly Business School of Nantes,
- Jean-Jacques Chanaron, Grenoble Ecole de Management,
- Dominique Jolly, formerly Ecole Superieure de Commerce Grenoble
- Oscar Marchisio, Studio Giano Bologna,
- Stephen Wood, London School of Economics,
- Ulrich Juergens, Science Center Berlin,
- Wolfgang Jahnke, Berlin University of Applied Science,
- Norbert Altmann, University of Bielefeld.

The author is convinced that all these friends recall the memories of the lectures at and their cooperation with Megatrend University. He is further sure that these friends are not hesitant to identify themselves with Megatrend University. To all of them, Megatrend University must be a symbol of *pioneering and creativity.* Without courage and creativity, this undertaking could not have overcome institutional, legal, financial and psychological barriers.

In this book, the author will discuss the system transformation in Serbia in the regional and global context. To be more precise, it deals with capacity-building in the process of transformation from socialist to capitalistic market economy in Serbia and also the question, to which extent young people educated at Megatrend University will be able to meet regional and global demand with their capability. In this respect, Mića Jovanović must have thought of *five* requirements of young people for being employed in a global company, as he expounded in his book "Business as Art of Living": *first*, work-oriented people replacing laziness; *second*, creative people not only for top-management, but also for executive part of a company; *third*, high-level education; *fourth*, loyalty to or identification with company goals; *fifth*, readiness to assess own capabilities and capacities. (Jovanović, 2008, pp 71-3)

Jovanović published a book in 2010 on the history of Megatrend University 1989-2009 entitled "The Mind Reigns". This book, as it is named, could be described as an embodiment of his *emotional and mindful inputs*. That is to say: a book on driving forces for Jovanović's Megatrend. The author is aware how important this emotional and mindful input was for Megatrend's success. As Winston Churchill once stressed in his speech (1943) at Harvard University, "the empires of the future will be *empires of the mind*".

Professors M. Jovanović, N. Masami i U. Juergens in Hiroshima, 1989.

Professors Mića Jovanović and Rebecca Morales at Sato Bridge, Japan, 1989.

Professors M. Jovanović, U. Juergens and Oscar Marchisio in Seoul 1989.

This book is to be understood as *a supplement* to the book "The Mind Reigns" which aims to bring some unknown stories and histories related to the creation and development of Megatrend University.

2. A Private University for System Transformation

2.1. Human Resources Development: from Marx to Kant

2.1.1. System Transformation: Gradualism or Crash Therapy

When '(system) transformation in former socialist economies' is concerned, there is a tendency to associate it with the 'crash therapy', as it has been carried out in Central and Eastern European countries. In most cases this approach resulted in a failure. Reflections on the failure were accompanied by the fact that as an alternative for the crash therapy, the gradual approach presupposing a relatively long transition period equivalent to preparing for a *take-off* towards transformation, has been gaining more importance in current policies and discussions. The gradual approach denotes a step-by-step effort, whereby the socialist economy, not being ready to dispense with communist party leadership, is still persistently leaning on central command. The case of the People's Republic of China proves this. In the Chinese case, the transformation has been pursued through properly proportioned hybridization of socialist and capitalist economy since the beginning of 1980s.

An important reflection on system transformation approach consists in taking historical, social, political, economic and cultural variables into consideration to change the socialist economy and political system in the country concerned (Seliger 2007), whereby a focus is to be placed on political actors. O'Donnell and Schmitter (1986) drew attention to the fact that it is quite possible to forecast which groups, persons, sectors, and institutions will play an important role in the transition period. However, it is still impossible to foretell what kind of interests will be manifested in those persons', groups' and institutions' behaviors and actions. Therefore, it is not clear at all whether any of them can be expected to exercise a coherent collective action for a successful transformation.

According to O'Donnell and Schmitter (1986), the system transformation requires two phases: the first phase is characterized by a change in political regime, installation of new political procedures, and securing of formal rights and obligations in conjunction with modification of social and economic conditions. (Oh 2007) But the time horizon of the shift from the first phase to the second cannot be specified exactly. However, in the second phase, the economic, social and political integration can be strived for and achieved as a result of the efficiently functioning market economy and democracy. Radosevic (2004) is propitiously referring to the importance of global aspects, by which the first phase and the second phase are differentiated as 'institutional transformation suitable for functioning market economy', and 'integration into global production and technology network' respectively. Nevertheless, no mention was made on the time dimension of transformation. Particularly, the role of human resources was not referred to either.

2.1.2. Human Resources Development in Transformation and Cluster Approach:

Experiences with transformation in former socialist economies indicate that the success of transformation is dependent on how much human beings are made amenable to dealing with the market economy. This means human resources getting familiar with market-relevant consciousness, attitudes, and behaviors in tandem with the transformation of legal, institutional, and organizational infrastructures. Meske (2004) emphasizes the necessity of *synchronic* consideration of all aspects of system transformation, as he states, "the starting point of system transformation lay in the political system but it then unfolded more or less simultaneously in the various subsystems. This gave rise less to simple cause and effect relationships than to a diversity of interrelationships". (Meske 2004, p.51)

Oh (2007) in charge of training and re-qualifying manpower in public sector of former socialist economies at the Asia Development Institute of Seoul National University proposed the following *cluster approach* for a successful transformation.

The insight into necessity of the *cluster approach* comes especially from the experiences of transformation in East Germany. In case of East Germany, seen from the standpoint of legal, institutional, and organizational infrastructures, the unification was carried out without significant impediments. Also, the financing of the unification could be easily arranged by means of the so called *solidarity pact*. The difficult problem, however, consisted in shortage of capitalistic rationality-inculcated manpower in factories, administration and other social and political organizations. Especially, decisions related to privatization of state-owned companies managed by the Treuhandanstalt in East Germany suffered to a large extent from lack of trained and experienced experts. For a certain time, West German delegates had to help East Germans in problem-solving as well as project planning and implementation in public sector. To be short, one of the most decisive problems in system transformation in East Germany was to have qualified and skilled manpower *on the spot*.

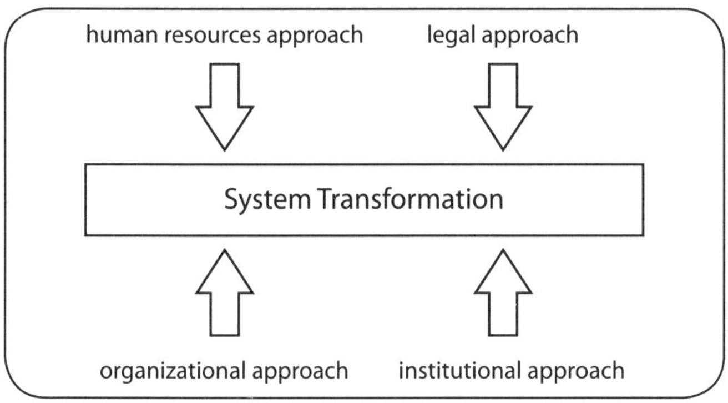

2.1.3. Self-Management Versus a New Human Resources Management

Mića Jovanović had already dealt with analysis of the self-management-in-use in former Yugoslavia and Serbia since 50s back in 80s and 90s. We cite his words: "the substance of free associated producers is social collective ownership over the means of production, instead of state ownership monopoly which existed (and still existing) in the socialist states of real socialism". (Jovanović 1991, p.91 f.) "...Basic organization of associated labour (BOAL) is the basic unit of each company". According to the Yugoslav Constitution (article 13) in all self-managed organization, the worker formally has the right to work with socially-owned means of production...

in order to satisfy personal and social needs and to manage his work, work conditions and the results of his labor freely and on equal footing with other workers in associated labour". (op.cit) Jovanović added that in the period of 1949-1979, the general economic condition was favorable and had a positive impact on performance of companies. However, since 1980, the situation of self-management changed. With one-sided increase in wealth and educational level, self-managers got estranged from workers and became bureaucratized 'officials' in companies. This led to decrease in motivation, discipline and labor productivity of the workers.

Referring to the case of "Yugo-America" production line with self-management, Mića Jovanović pointed out the discrepancy between non-materialistic, institutionally and legally provided rights and materialistic incentives. In case of the reform of industrial relations, considering self-management as 'moral order' may be plausible. However, tangible productivity increase from the side of workers could be expected, according to Jovanović, only if monetary incentive was given for self-management.

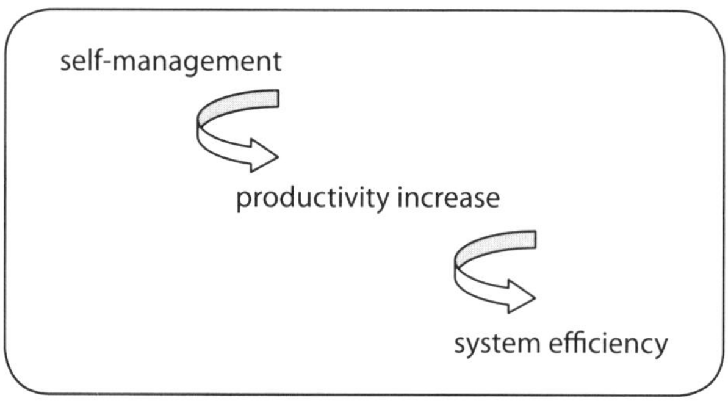

Self-Management concept (based on central command)

Around 1990, the self-management was suspended by the new government. Critical reflections on self-management were necessitated for transformation of socialist into market economy. Mića Jovanović's contribution to discussions on which strategy should be chosen in Serbia was remarkable: Stating at the end of his critical essay on self-management "Business and self-management are not linked", he emphatically stressed, "even more business should be going to overwhelm self-management in Yugoslavia". (Jovanović.op.cit, p.102). He clearly underlined the necessity of influencing workforce by means of calculative rationality.

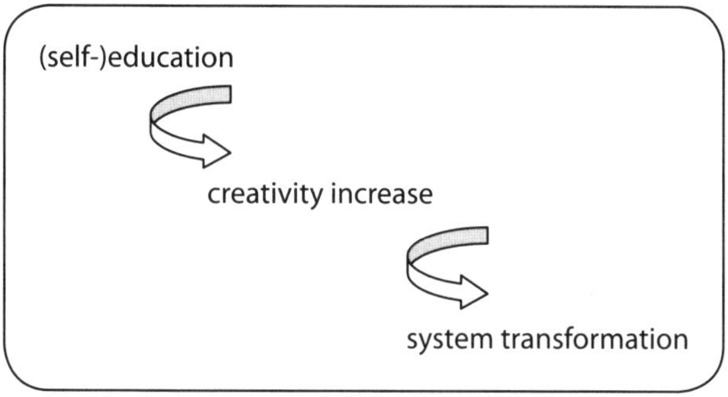

Mića Jovanović's Megatrend concept
(based on individual, private, decentral initiative)

Mića Jovanović who enjoyed his management education in UK was armed with expertise on Western management theories, especially Japanese lean production system, Volvo production system, and German co-determination. During his study in London, he was already successful in establishing *a global experts pool* around him consisting of Profs. Juergens and Park (Berlin), Abo, Sei, Ikeda (Japan), etc. He studied the cause of the so-called 'Japanese and Korean miracle' with great admiration and came to the conclusion of placing heaviest accent on *human resources* for sustainable organizational and institutional efficiency.

Japan and Korea have offered an excellent example in success of human resources development. Jovanović's notion was, as Kant said, necessity of *relying on ratio* (for enlightenment) instead of accent on workers' solidarity a la Marx, and then reaching a stage where 'we are grown-up and do not need guardians (Vormundschaft)'. The question for transforming a system is how to raise an autonomous, grown-up personality through education to increase self-confidence in capacity and action. (see the picture on next page)

Let us compare the self-management and Mića Jovanović's notion on human resources development:

1. The self-management started to flourish in the period of Tito's socialism, when the so-called grass roots workers' management participation was *idealized*. In theory, the self-management's ideology aligns with Japanese lean management, German co-determination and Swedish Volvo management with regard to how to reduce negative impact on morale and motivation of workforce resulting from *fordistic mass production*. That

was the reason why many scholars, especially union-friendly experts in the West welcomed this self-management system. *In practice*, however, the self-management resulted in bureaucratization of intra-organizational decision-making which caused decrease in workers' labor motivation and productivity. Mića Jovanović's concept, however, aimed at the question of how 'new type' of human resources should be developed in conjunction with the system transformation in a country like Serbia. The 'new type' of human resources implied *continuous education and re-qualification* (tantamount to the Japanese Kaizen) of young people who were not used to the self-management. Since the system transformation in Serbia had to be carried out in corporation with profit-oriented capitalistic enterprises by means of foreign direct investments, the 'new type' of human resources had to be developed as soon as possible in order to meet *demand for business- and open-minded young people accustomed to western modern managerial methods.*

2. In terms of differences in *incentive system,* the self-management stressed 'moral order' and legal and institutional-political incentives for workforce, while Jovanović's intention consisted in development of *creative potential* tailored towards globally operating companies.

3. The self-management was created by the central government and practiced upon strict central regulations. Jovanović's concept mainly dealt with *private* companies, whose major part was likely to be of foreign origin sooner or later in Serbia. It was important that Jovanović's concept aimed at enhancing *individual creativity,* whereas the self-management regarded *group/collective solidarity* to be more significant.

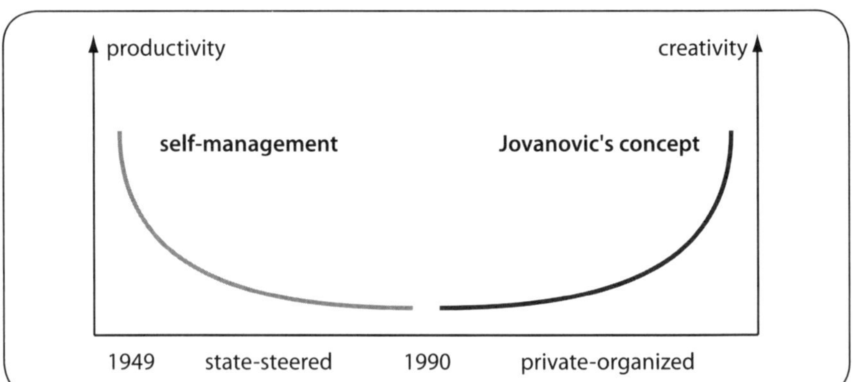

Self-Management versus Jovanović's concept

2.1.4. *Knowledge Economy and Lifestyle:*

Looking at this picture, it is visible that the system transformation in Serbia first began in 1990. Indications, such as productivity decrease of workforce, have shown the sign of the collapse of self-management around this time. Foreseeing that the self-management would result in a failure sooner or later, Jovanović prepared for the future of Serbia in London by building up a human resources-oriented organization entitled "Megatrend International Expert Consortium" which was to act as a starting point of global talent pool in the future. Here, he has shown his talent to think of something new and act, as it is needed. This "expert consortium" could be named 'global talent pool' in current terms which was to be utilized as a propitious instrument for his future university.

Reading his very recent book "Business as Art of Living", one can trace back to the beginning of 80s, when nobody talked about "megatrend" (three years later, Mr. Naisbitt used it for the first time). Jovanović allegedly reserved this expression for the knowledge economy which formed the background for entitlement of the current university. The question is: what was his perception about the knowledge economy? He more broadly perceived the concept of 'knowledge' introduced in 60s by Fritz Machlup (1962) who understood it as a correlation between industrial production and distribution. Jovanović went with his above-mentioned book far beyond Fritz Machlup and touched on the question of how the tertiary economy can be combined with knowledge economy, to be more concrete, how the lifestyle-based service economy can reach higher value-creation in the knowledge economy. He tried to give an answer with the following formula.

$$DI = \Sigma e / \Sigma y$$

(DI: intensity of life; sigma e - sigma event; sigma y - sigma year)

According to him, DI (intensity of life) stands for "creative way to prolong life", event "e" implying organization and management to effectively pursue lifestyle, and year "y" meaning sustainability of lifestyle. We may ask how DI comprehends the service economy which is to be linked to elaboration of widening and deepening effects of lifestyle, where the knowledge economy can be instrumental. Probably, Jovanović must have sought for the answer when accelerating the project Megatrend University.

2.2. Global Talent Pool

"All of us committed ourselves to Mića's idea to embark on a new private university".

(Prof. Oscar Marchisio, Studio Giano Bologna)

2.2.1. Three Big Events in 1989

2.2.1.1. Consilience and Multiculturalism

Building up a global talent pool in knowledge economy is nowadays an essential globalization strategy at governmental and corporate level. One has been using the word "War for Talent", or "Hunting for High Level Manpower" in connection with a global talent pool. Most advanced countries and MNCs have been concurrently making attempts to set up a global talent pool. What does this mean? It means assembling a group of highly qualified experts with excellent, specialized knowledge, and experiences in a systemic network which is regarded as an essential instrument for a regional knowledge economy.

For realizing this idea, the following requirements must be fulfilled:

- acceptance of multi-culturalism and creation of tolerant society
- experiences in getting along with foreign experts
- competence in foreign languages
- facilitation of immigration regulations, especially for those who come from Third World
- existence of regional industrial policy aimed at transforming industrial economy into knowledge economy

Richard Florida (2002) who coined out the terminology 'creative class' referred to three requirements for formation of creative class in the USA: *technology, talent and tolerance* (*Florida's 3 Ts*). The tolerance defined by Florida implies not only multiculturalism, but also acceptance of gays, and hippies, and also so called social dissidents and isolated people. The notion of tolerance may further denote amalgamation of different races and cultures which is true in case of the Balkan region characterized by traditional *melting pot of different races, cultures, nationalities and religions.*

The multiculturalism of Megatrend University is later reflected in *diversity* of detachment localities of Megatrend University and *multiplicity* of university cooperation partners in global context. The typical example for localization diversity is Zajecar's Megatrend Business School (Higher Management School) which is located close to the Bulgarian and Romanian borders convenient for receiving students from Bulgaria and Romania. The other example of multiplicity of university cooperation partnerships is Megatrend's joining in NEWS and EAMSA at the very early stage. Both associations will be extensively touched on later.

Jovanović was convinced of importance of the global talent pool at the beginning of his career and began with the opening of a knowledge-based academic network entitled "Megatrend International Expert Consortium Ltd." in London in 1980. The aim of this organization was to pursue exchange of talents beyond nationality, race, and culture, and to run business in terms of global talent hunting and lastly to utilize talented people for his future university. His pioneering undertaking with this project seemed to offer a model for future-looking strategy of knowledge economy. In Serbia, only few might have understood the real implication of "Megatrend International Expert Consortium". Even his close friends did not presumably understand its implications.

Jovanović commented on the International Expert Consortium: "Something completely new in Yugoslavia in the late 1980s was the *service called knowledge*. It was necessary to make a good concept and to appear first on the market". (Jovanović 2008, p.226)

The following experts were available for Jovanović's university project. They accompanied the pre-Megatrend in that they were invited regularly to give lectures on updated developments in various disciplines and consultancy related to development of a new university in connection with system transformation. The following scholars were standing for a colorful diversity as regards profound research and long teaching experiences.

- *Abo Tetsuo,* Tokyo University (International Economy)
- *Norbert Altmann*, University of Bielefeld/Sozialwissenschaftliches Institut Muenchen (Industrial Sociology)

- *Galen Amstutz*, Harvard University (Cultural Anthropology and Sociology of Religion)
- *Jean-Jacques Chanaron*, Grenoble Graduate School of Management (Industrial and Labor Economics)
- *Sam Dzever*, Universite de Nantes (Management Science and Supply Chain Management)
- *Andras Hernadi*, Hungarian Academy of World Economy (International Economy)
- *Ikeda Masao*, Chuo University (Automotive Industry)
- *Ulrich Juergens,* Free University Berlin/Wissenschaftszentrum Berlin (Political Economy of Industrial Relations)
- *Kim Byongsub*, Seoul National University (Public Administration)
- *Sung-Jo Park,* Free University Berlin/President of Euro-Asia Management Studies Association (Industry Economy and Industrial Relations)
- *Oscar Marchisio*, Studio Giano and University of Genoa (Automotive Industry)
- *Nomura Masami*, Okayama University (Labor Economics)
- *Rebecca Morales*, University of California, Los Angeles (Regional Economy)
- *Arthur Stockwin,* Oxford University (Political Science and International Relations)
- *Stephen Wood*, London School of Economics and Political Science (Industrial Relations)
- *Johan Galtung,* Transcend Paris (Peace Research)
- *Grishka Bogdanoff,* University of Bourgogne (Mathematics)
- *Igor Bogdanoff,* University of Bourgogne (Mathematics)
- *Hugh Montgomery,* Grand Commander, Order of the Fleur-de-Lys (European History)
- *Dominique Jolly,* CERAM, Sophia Antipolis, Nice (Human Resource Management)
- *Michel Polski,* Grenoble Graduate School of Management
- *Thierry Grange,* Grenoble Graduate School of Management (R&D Management)
- *William K. Holstein,* State University of New York
- *Tim Morris,* London Business School
- *Geoffrey Darnton,* Bournemouth University (Computer Sciences, IT)

- *Alain Buzelay,* Pantheon Sorbonne, University Paris I
- *Charlotte Riedberger,* Académie de Psychoanalyse Paris (Psychology).

The composition of these scholars and experts was *multi-disciplinary,* characterized by abundant experiences and high level expertise in their own field. Economics, management science, anthropology, political science, physics, peace research, mathematics, philosophy etc. were represented. Scholars had different nationalities, coming from the USA, UK, France, Germany, Japan, Norway, Korea, Hungary, Italy, etc. The easily noticeable merkmal of Jovanović's global talent pool was to form a yardstick for his later university!

2.1.1.2. Mića Jovanović: Personality and Expertise

How was it possible that Jovanović succeeded in gathering so many renowned scholars and experts around him? Did he simply have luck?, or did he entice them by means of financial compensation? His gravitation came from other sources: *One* important factor was academic expertise of Mića Jovanović and his personality. Scarcely had he finished his Ph.D. at London School of Economic and Political Science, then became he soon Professor at Universities in UK and advisor for Zastava car factory production. His personality is open, modest, diligent and had no difficulty in making friendship with people with other nationalities. His adaptability to different conditions was absolutely his strength. He is extremely sensitive to finding something new and special.

The *other* momentum was that the Yugo car reached a great market sale in the USA in a very short period despite severe competition with the Korean car "Pony". The difference between them was that Yugo was made on the basis of *autonomous* technology in Serbia, while Pony was a product of Mitsubishi's technology. Experts worldwide were greatly interested to know more details about the Yugo car. Mića Jovanović had a profound expertise on Yugo car's production system and therefore he appeared at many prominent places as expert in Yugo car production. Further, his dissertation on self-management in Yugoslavia was an additional attraction, because he could convincingly argue the upcoming collapse of self-management with immeasurable courage under the Tito socialism.

His argument on inefficiency in productivity of self-management took an unconventional position against euphemistically represented opinions by most scholars in Serbia in favor of the self-management. There were many admirers of self-management worldwide among young generation. Jovanović did not cease to allude to inefficiency of self-management, wherever he had chance in Europe, Japan, Korea and the USA. He stressed a plea repeatedly for a substantial change of self-management for system transformation.

Jovanović's intention went far beyond the mentioned criticism on self-management. The substantial reason for his argument was this: He understood human-being (workforce) as *production factor not perfectly made* for efficiency. His notion was to begin the system transformation by means of making "new human-beings" for efficiency. To pinpoint the difference between two concepts, the concept of self-management is based on workforce partout productive *sui generis*, whilst Jovanović's concept stems from 'imperfect human-being' whose productivity and creativity can be *enhanced by means of education*. This juxtaposition is also true for the difference between socialism and capitalism in general sense.

Jovanović's friends from USA, East Asia and various European academic top-institutions were strongly impressed by his idea. They firmly decided to help Mića Jovanović realize his project "Megatrend". *Megatrend was thus conceived of as an international joint undertaking by friends built on Schumpeterian spirit. Without taking this spirit of international solidarity into proper consideration, Megatrend University's identity could not be grasped in a sufficient way.* The fact that Mića Jovanović took the path nobody went before him inspired his friends. This was the attraction for them to take part in the Megatrend Project.

To his personality, especially his diligence has to be added. As the following list of his publications (here only books) shows, Mića Jovanović has been restlessly writing books and articles.

- Sociology of Self-Management (Belgrade, 1980)
- 69 Lessons on Management (Belgrade 1991)
- Intercultural Management (Belgrade 2001)
- Works Motivation and Self-Management (London 2002)
- Strategic Management (co-author, Belgrade 1990)

- What is behind the Japanese Miracle? (Co-editor, London-Berlin-Tokyo, 1995)
- Organizational Behavior (co-author, Belgrade 1999)
- Strategic Management (co-author, Belgrade 2001)
- Project Management (co-author, Belgrade 2001)
- Organizational Behavior (co-author, Belgrade 2003)
- Intercultural Challenges of Globalization (co-author, Belgrade 2006)
- Before the Big Bang (co-author, Belgrade-Paris 2006)
- Business as Art of Living (Belgrade 2008)
- The Mind Reigns. History of the Megatrend University 1989-2009 (Belgrade 2010).

2.2.1.3. *Jovanović's debut in Berlin, Seoul, and Tokyo: Globalization of Car Industry and Production Management*

Jovanović's first noteworthy international debut was his presentation on production system and self-management of the Yugo car factory at the International Automobile Conference hosted by the Berlin Wissenschaftszentrum (WZB) (hoster: Prof. Ulrich Juergens) in 1988. Almost all automobile experts and scholars came together in Berlin for three days. His contribution made a great impression on scholars from abroad. Promptly, an invitation came from South Korea. This country was at that time aiming to become one of the 6 biggest car makers in the world.

Mića Jovanović in front of the Seoul Hilton.

On May 15-16, 1989, the International Conference on *Technology, Labor, and Labor Relations* was held by KAMA (Korea Automobile Manufacturers Association) in conjunction with Seoul National University. Korea as a newcomer in automotive industry was enthusiastic to learn from advanced car-manufacturing countries, and also ambitious to align with them in car production in the near future. At that time, the newly established KAMA asked the author who had long experiences in advising Volkswagen since the beginning 80s to organize an automotive industry conference in Korea. The people and organizations in Korea did not know who was working where on what. The author with a fresh memory on the Berlin Conference had a good hand in choosing excellent speakers from different countries. The conference made a well-balanced impression as regards academic representation of all important car producing countries in the world. The two-day conference in a big hall of Hilton Hotel Seoul covering more than 700 participants was a great success. The Minister of Industry and Commerce, Prof. Han Sung-Su welcomed all speakers. The panel discussion was moderated by the renowned economist, Prof. Park Woo-Hee, Seoul National University, currently rector of Sejong University in Seoul.

The Plan of the Conference had the following contents:

Introduction by Sung-Jo Park, Berlin

- Prospects of the World Automotive Industry in the 1990s

New Technology and Manpower

- *Jean Jacques Chanaron, Grenoble*
  New Concepts of Work Groups and Work Organization in the French Car Industry
- *Oscar Marcisio, Milano*
  Technological Innovation and Emergence of the Real Organization in the Assembly of the Tipo at the Fiat Casino
- *Mića Jovanović, Belgrade*
  "The Business of the Century": the De-coupling of Business and Self-Management

New Technology and Labor Relations

- *Rebecca Morales, Los Angeles*
  Work Organization, Technology and Labor Relations in the US Automobile Industry
- *Ulrich Juergens, Berlin*
  New Technology, Work Organization and Industrial Relations in the Federal Republic of Germany
- *Stephen Wood, London*
  Developments in the British Car Industry in the Mid-Eighties

Japanese Strategies

- *Tetsuo Abo, Tokyo*
  New Technology and Manpower Utilization in Japanese Automobile Firms in Japan and their Plants in the United States
- *Masayoshi Ikeda, Tokyo*
  The Transfer of Flexible Production System to Japanese auto parts maker transplants in the US.

The resonance of this conference was enormous. The former CEO of Hyundai Automobile Plant, Mr. Jung Mong-Ku (graduate from Korea University and Oxford) said once "that Conference was the best one that I have ever experienced in Korea".

Unfortunately, after this conference, no other workshop of this kind was held in Korea.

It was difficult to bring renowned experts of car industry together. The author was lucky to find those experts who were advising this or that car maker in their home country:

- Jean-Jacques Chanaron for Renault,
- Stephen Wood for Rover,
- Oscar Marchisio for Fiat,
- Abo Tetsuo for Toyota,
- Ikeda Masayoshi for Nissan,
- Ulrich Jurgens for Volkswagen,
- Mića Jovanović for Zastava,
- Rebecca Morales for Ford
- Park Sung-Jo for Volkswagen and Kia.

The communication at the Conference in Seoul was of great help for Korean experts involved in car manufacturing. Most audiences who never had a chance to get familiar with other advanced car industry were pleased to learn about an overview of all advanced car-manufacturing countries. The proceedings of this Conference was published in 1991 by Campus Frankfurt/New York with the title: Sung-Jo Park (ed.) "Technology and Labor in the Automotive Industry" (Campus: Frankfurt/New York).

Professor Jean-Jacques Chanaron

When Korea embarked on car production about 30 years ago, most experts compared it with 'a flash in the pan'. The study results by the MIT Automobile Study Group, in particular, the book *"The machine that changed the world"(1990; Womack, Jones and Roos)* which highly lauded the Japanese way of car production (Toyota production system), attributed no premium on the Korean car industry, because Koreans have been known for lack of production technology, experiences, manpower and financial resources and also of marketing knowhow. The repeated prognosis by the MIT Automobile Study Group that the Korean Car Industry would not reach prosperity was in a striking contrast with its current success worldwide.

For Mića Jovanović, who was very familiar with the production of Yugo car, the expedition to East Asia was extremely instrumental in many respects: *first*, his trip to Fat East, a region which is culturally and mentally completely different from Europe, enabled him to get in touch with the Asian culture and mentality; *second*, he had a chance to visit the Hyundai Car Plant in Ulsan (Korea) and the Toyota Motors Co in Nagoya (Japan). For the first time, he came physically in contact with the 'Asian way of production management'. Here, the 'Asian' meant Toyota production system. Hyundai, the Korean car maker already adopted the Toyota production system with a multiple sub-contracting tier system in culminating in Just-In-Production (JIT); *third*, he could fulfill his special wish to visit some subcontractors. Since the author had served as advisor for Korean Auto Manufacturers Association (KAMA), he knew many subcontractors. He chose a special subcontractor among manufacturing condensers for Hyundai, named "Myungwha Co. Ltd". This company's production technology came from Germany and at that time it just began to supply partly to Mercedes Benz and Volkswagen. Mića Jovanović visited this company located near Seoul. He could see how workers in groups were working at shop level. In the evening, he was invited to a special Korean dinner by the president of Myungwha Co. Ltd.

Juergens, Morales, Ikeda, Abo, Jovanović, Marchisio...
at Seoul Conference in 1989.

In Japan, he could also visit some Toyota subcontractors guided by Prof. Nomura (Okayama University). His conclusion had been that the group work was "autonomous, creative, and making suggestions" (Kaizen); *lastly*, he could get in touch personally with Mr. Jung Se-Young, former president of Hyundai Car Plant (he died some years ago), while Mr. Jung was hosting a dinner for all speakers of the Seoul Conference in the restaurant of the '63 floors Building'. Mića Jovanović was asked by Mr. Jung to deliver a speech on behalf of all Conference speakers. He did two things, first a speech, and second, he played on guitar while singing. It was really a big fun for all attendants.

Jovanović, Morales, Juergens... In Toyota, 1989.

2.2.2. *Pre-Megatrend Era*

2.2.2.1. First Steps towards Megatrend University: Improvisation and Pragmatism

The year of 1989 was very significant for Prof. Mića Jovanović, because he started with the first concrete move to build up Megatrend University. The beginning was made with a small institute located on the first floor in a high building, downtown of Belgrade, comprising 6 staff, some office facilities and a handful of hundred students founded on Dec. 27, 1989. Megatrend University has been celebrating this date as its birthday. In those days, the author tried to be with Mića Jovanović as frequently as possible, because the author got the feeling: Mića needs someone to talk to very frankly. One day, he called the author in Berlin: There will be a big event for celebrating the first decade birthday of Megatrend University. The festivity was held in a very big theatre, downtown of Belgrade with prominent guests from education, science, politics, business world, and arts and music. The high ranking politicians such as Minister of Education, Minister of Foreign Affairs, President of Serbian Parliament, etc. and prominent scholars such as the President of Serbian Academy of Sciences, were present there. Finally, the author was asked to appear on the stage and say something in celebration of Megatrend University. According to his memory, the author must have said: "All of us are witnessing how Mića Jovanović and Serbia make a new history". After the celebration was over, some professors, Mića Jovanović and the author moved to other relatively small, but very noble hall. About 40 professors were already there where a festivity of conferring an honorary doctorate degree in Economics on the author began. The author was lucky to be accompanied by his student from Serbia studying at Free University Berlin. She could translate everything for him. The chairman of the Trustee Board of Megatrend University first read its resolution to confer the honorary doctorate degree on the author. The author was very pleased to receive this great honor. This was the first honorary doctorate degree granted by Megatrend University. Then the chairman asked the author to give a talk on "The future of American Finance Capital-centered Globalization".

Around these years, Jovanović needed more help than before from his colleagues abroad. Jovanović did not give up his firm conviction that he and Megatrend University can rely on his friends abroad to support his idea to establish a new type of university in Serbia. He regularly invited '7 colleagues' ('big 7'), and case by case some other experts. In the case of lectures for companies such as Smederevo Steel Mill, Energoinvest Sarajevo, Bor Mining Co., etc., Jovanović preferred to invite those experts versed in management techniques aimed at contributing to directly improving productivity of workplace. But in the case of general managers and bankers as well as other clienteles (lawyers, accountants, tax consultants, travel agencies, etc.), those experts familiar with International Economy and

Trade, Peace Research, International Politics etc. were preferred as sourcing persons. This resilient utilization of experts by Jovanović was possible thanks to the already mentione d *global experts pool*. For instance, utilizing the global experts pool Jovanović had a good hand: those experts more versed in management techniques were delegated to companies located in local towns such as Novi Sad, Kragujevac, Bor, etc., and others with expertise in current international business and economy appeared in manager training and re-qualifying seminars held in Belgrade.

Professor Park with the golden medal of Honorary Doctoral Degree and his student from the Berlin Free University, 27th of December 1999 (10th Anniversary of Megatrend University).

The other problem Jovanović confronted at the beginning was to secure spaces for the administration and lecture rooms. His office moved to many places renting unused spaces and rooms in old buildings in the downtown of Belgrade. The lectures were held at sparsely located places in downtown, sometime in theatres, halls of labor unions and banks, and spaces affiliated with the Belgrade City Administration. Also, facilities and lecture-supporting tools were in an extremely miserable condition. Nowadays, the use of power-point presentation is common at Megatrend University, but at that time even overhead projectors were not available. Microphones were also in a very poor quality. Additionally, attendants of lectures were not able to understand English, so most lectures were dependent on interpreters. Jovanović was fortunate to have excellent professors at English department who were very useful by providing translation at this stage. Nevertheless, whenever and wherever lectures took place, the space was always full of attendants. One had to notice how serious the hunger of people for new information and knowledge was. All these poor facilities and conditions now belong to the past. The facilities in the current main building (Goce Delceva Street 8, 11070 Belgrade) and the building with the faculty of arts are far beyond international standard. Teaching conditions are in high international standard. Facilities are excellent and all university institutes are easily accessible. One can notice easily how much importance Mića Jovanović attributed to university infrastructures. As regards locational choice of university institute complex, he seems to have taken into consideration which part of Belgrade would gain more importance in new settlement planning of the Belgrade City in the future. The university is now located in the new town of Belgrade which has an easy access to the highways and the international airport.

2.2.2.2. New Management Principles and Techniques

The author belonged to those experts group expected to primarily teach management techniques, being mainly involved in plants under the system of socialist economy and self-management such as Bor Mining, Smederevo Steel Company, Energoinvest, etc. In those companies, one did not know exactly, firstly, how to *evaluate* individual's and group's performance, and, secondly, how to precisely *switch* results of measured performance *to* wage determination and promotion.

The lectures the author gave at Bor Mining Co., Smederevo Steel Company, etc. focused on personnel appraisal and performance wage determination and promotion, for which he mostly used Toyota management techniques and adapted them to Serbian local conditions. The author already collected experiences in application of Toyota management techniques to firms in Germany, for instance Volkswagen. Most attendants of his lectures were responsible for personnel and labor management.

The subjects were related to exercise of various model calculations. The author got impression that attendants understood techniques very quickly. However, they confessed that the introduction of new management techniques in companies was not a problem of understanding by workforce, but how to persuade and convince labor representatives persistently adhering to self-management of greater efficiency of lean management and group work system. Nevertheless, all participants exercised and experimented with personnel and performance appraisal under the leadership of the author. However, he had no chance to check later how and to which extent these new techniques had been familiarized in local companies. He still thinks that a follow-up study on the learning by Serbian workforce of management techniques would be recommendable.

The other group of experts consisted of Juergens (Berlin), Nomura (Japan), Abo (Japan) Morales (Los Angeles), Chanaron (Grenoble) and Ikeda (Japan). With these experts, mostly two-day seminars were organized in the Beograder International Congress Center. The seminar of this kind in 1989/1990 was attracting executives, lawyers, tax consultants, travel agencies, etc. Later Jovanović stated that "first steps in the education…. should be made, since the changes in the economy of Yugoslavia had started, which were to include it in European and world trends". (Jovanović. op.cit. p.22)

Japanese colleagues were very familiar with details of management techniques. For instance, Profs. Ikeda, Abo and Nomura having long experiences in consultancy in Japan and abroad were extremely instrumental for attendants. Japanese colleagues, particularly Prof. Ikeda (Chuo University) are internationally well-known experts in personnel and labor management, because they pursued personnel performance appraisal by Japanese firms investing in different countries such as UK, Germany, the USA and Korea. The problem with these experts was a long-way flight to come to Belgrade. Despite this inconvenience, Japanese colleagues bore burdensome travel to Belgrade.

Profs. Juergens, Chanaron and Morales were known as automobile experts. Since at that time, the Yugo car industry was about to gain worldwide broad acceptance, in particular in the USA, executives, experts and scholars concerned with the Yugo car industry were enthusiastic to learn about new trends of major car makers such as Volkswagen, Renault and Ford. It was said that their expertise and information on German, French and American car industry were very valuable for the Yugo car industry, since the Serbian car industry under the socialist economy remained isolated for a long time from the western car industry.

2.2.3. The Bosnian Crisis, Bombings and Friendships

2.2.3.1. *Import of Western Management School and Decentralized Dissemination of Management Techniques*

Scarcely had Jovanović begun gradually with materializing his idea, then was he faced with very severe hindrances caused by the Bosnian War, UN embargo policy and NATO bombings. Serbia was nearly completely cut from the outward world, being driven into an isolation.

However, Jovanović took this difficult situation as a challenge just like the Chinese term: the *crisis* means a *new opportunity*. The most serious difficulty entailed by the Bosnian Crisis was that his international connections were threatened to break down. However, he did not despair and continued to hold management seminars with the above-mentioned foreign experts, above all, Jean-Jacques Chanaron and the author.

When organizing seminars with foreign experts, Jovanović gave premium on local towns. He spared no effort, driving foreign lecturers by his jeep to various local towns. From these local towns, later detachments of Megatrend University, such as Zajecar's Megatrend Business School were born. He also played the role of being an interpreter. It was very interesting that the atmosphere of seminars with Jovanović as interpreter was quite different from that of those seminars in which so-called professional interpreters did translations. In such cases, a more or less mechanical translation was carried out, whilst Jovanović's interpretation contained additional and critical comments on the same topics, because he completely understood the connotation of lectures. Thus, his interpretation was 'explaining' and 'discursive' that enabled audience to understand new management principles and techniques very easily. It was different when Jovanović employed some so-called professional interpreters. They were not accustomed to special terminologies in management and international business e.g. lean production, QC circle, Kaizen, Just-In-Time, TQC, etc. and particularly to very new management technique-related terminologies such as Balanced Scorecard, Supply Chain Management. Therefore, it was not clear to which extent the contents of lectures were really understood by the audience.

The author stressed frequently that one could not ignore cultural specificity in management techniques, even though there has been an increasing trend toward standardization and uniformitization. Anyhow, Jovanović's interpretation capability was highly appreciated. But nobody knows how long Jovanović did this interpretation job. Maybe at least 5-6 years! Later, he employed some interpreters. The author thought sometime that Mića Jovanović must be omnipotent!

By holding many seminars with foreign experts, Mića Jovanović attempted to bring new management methods and techniques as well as most recent globalization-relevant information to local areas in order to keep new teaching programs from being concentrated solely in Belgrade. Jovanović's decentral dissemination of new management methods and techniques had a decisive influence on his university detachments. On top of it, expertise and information about updated management theories and techniques brought into Serbia must have given Mića Jovanović much confidence in his strategy to *"set up something new in Serbia"*. The author was often told by seminar participants that management techniques introduced in seminars were absolutely new to Serbia. Jovanović represented the position that at that time a sort of paradigm change in management principles and techniques was taking place worldwide and, above all, the young generation should be accustomed to these new things to keep pace with young students in the West. Without exaggeration, this fact made Mića Jovanović 'exceptional' in Serbia and the Balkan region in the sense of bringing new expertise and information which was of a great value for capacity-building in the transformation process. That is to say, Mića Jovanović must have played the role of being a messenger of 'new management'. Otherwise, the author is not able to explain why he received so many orders from famous big companies.

Jovanović's insight to accentuate *local* interests and *local* specificity did not depend simply on his local origin, but had recourse to his dealing with the West German concept of transformation which overwhelmed the East German economy: He saw a serious dilemma in East Germany was in that there was a great deal of shortage of experts in handling local development in a proper way of transforming socialist economy into capitalist economy in local productive entities. The shortage of local experts in East Germany led to import of western so called 'transformation experts' who did not consider local needs and interests in East Germany. It was said that these experts sometime did not understand local mentality and local specificity.

Experiences in former socialist economies taught a lesson that a structural reform in the socialist economy has to be *gradually* pursued, instead of 'crash'-strategy, as it has been the case in Russia, Poland, East Germany etc.; lastly, locally spread still-existing small handicraft and industrial small firms in Serbia should be adapted gradually to capitalistic market behaviors. Above these approaches, the following pre-condition is important that experts familiar with local sensibility and specificity should be available *on the spot*, which was very seriously lacking at the beginning of industrial transformation in East Germany.

Additionally, Mića Jovanović was greatly skeptical of mechanic transfer of Western capitalism to Serbia. Jovanović and the author discussed the question of what kind of capitalism could be more suitable for Serbia. Without finding a concrete answer, both shared the opinion on that the Western capitalism, European or American, which undoubtedly brought forth enormous success in the past, is likely to be not competitive enough to counter future Asian capitalisms such as Chinese, Japanese and others, which were not relevant to the typology of capitalism by Michel Albert (1993), and by Hall and Soskice (2001). That was the reason why it was from the beginning on Jovanović's notion to deal with emerging economies such as China, India, and Southeast Asia that led later to the establishment of the Faculty of Geo-Economic Studies. This means, in fact, that the globalization should not be understood as simple diffusion of Western capitalism.

It was *ultimo ratio* for Mića Jovanović with a serious intention to set up a management school tailored towards tackling *specific problems* of Serbian system transformation. As regards this, there are two concurrent positions. The *one* position shared by most experts is that it is sufficient enough to rely on Western economic/management theories from Europe and the USA. The *other* position is that it is very likely that the economic hegemony by the USA and Europe would eclipse in a foreseeable future. Unfortunately, the first position is broadly represented by Western experts lacking ability to see the world development in a rather differentiated and far-reaching way. The author was reminded often of the fact that the Western economic hegemony would be over sooner or later and instead, the Asian and Pacific region would be playing a dominant role in the world economy. Considering this fact, Jovanović found a solution in *consilience* of different capitalisms based on a variety of cultures and on experiences with capitalism in other countries.

It is regrettable that lots of former socialist economies suffering lack of capitalistic-trained managers hurried up to allow foreign firms and business schools to open management school without prior profound scrutiny about adaptability of new management principles and techniques to completely different local environments. Everywhere in former socialist economies, business schools were concurrently opened attracting young people which incurred high education investment. These schools were established often motivated by profit-making of Western businessmen. A typical case is China. Management experts in China refer to the fact that in former time, a great admiration for the Western management system existed in China, but currently a hybridization of Western, Asian and local management system is increasingly gaining importance. That is the reason why Chinese-Foreign Business Schools are emerging in China one after another.

2.2.3.2. Personnel Appraisal and Performance Evaluation During NATO Bombings

Mića Jovanović has many friends abroad, as already said. However, this seemingly rosy friendship was exposed to probe, when the Bosnian War broke out in 1991. Most of his colleagues abroad expressed their unwillingness to continue support for Jovanović's project. They were apprehensive of *risking visit* to Serbia. They might have thought that Jovanivc's project would be doomed to a failure sooner or later. They declined coming for teaching at Megatrend during Bosnian War, since terrible battles were fought less than 100 kilometers west of Belgrade. But there were two exceptions: Prof. Chanaron and the author did not mind these risky circumstances and continued their support for Jovanović. That is probably the reason why Mića Jovanović often says: " Megatrend University survived the crisis and bombings thanks to the help by Chanaron and Park, thus it was built on three pillars such as Jovanović, Chanaron and Park".

2.2.3.2.1. Personnel Appraisal and Performance Evaluation

Due to the UN embargo, there was no flight connection between Belgrade and European cities. This meant: whenever Jovanović got orders from local companies to train and re-qualify managers, he asked Prof.

Chanaron and the author to reach first the Budapest Airport in order to come to Belgrade, because Budapest was the only airport for Serbians to go and to come from abroad.

The case of the author: He had to fly first from Berlin to Budapest and had to meet someone assigned by Mića Jovanović to pick him up at the Budapest Airport. In this case, the car driver drove the author by his car to Belgrade. But sometimes, he was instructed to take a seat in a minibus which transported about 5-6 other persons bound for Belgrade. The passport and customs control at the Hungarian-Serbian Border took usually 3-4 hours. After all these formalities, the author arrived at Belgrade around 6-7 o'clock in the morning. His lectures were to begin at 8:30 or 9 o'clock somewhere in barrack-like houses. Usually, more than 100 attendants, the young and old, were waiting for him. Since he was not able to speak Serbian, his lectures were mostly in English and had to be translated into Serbian. This meant: two hours for his lecture in the morning, then additional 2 hours and slightly longer with translation, as some questions came. Then, the lunch was around 1-2 o'clock.

After the lunch, his lecture was held in the same way as in the morning. In the evening, Mića Jovanović was waiting for the author in a restaurant. The dinner in Serbia was not simply to enjoy meal within a short time. It was a sort of friendly ceremony finalizing all things happened during the day.

The atmosphere with friends was usually very vivid and enjoyable. Serbian people loved singing songs together with some help of Serbian local brandy 'slivovitz' (plum brandy), whenever a chance was given. The author noticed soon that these songs had a melancholic rhythm which reminded him of East Asian songs.

The author's lectures were on performance evaluation of workforce and executives, grouped into individual, group and system performance. In particular, the application of personnel appraisal system was a problem, because most workforce and executives were not familiar with this system and showed apprehension over the use of it in their own organization. Concerning wage determination, it was necessary for all employees to get their own performance evaluated. Only with an objective evaluation of workforce's performance, one could determine the performance-based wage. This didn't seem plausible to many people because they used to have only seniority-based wage system and seniority-determined promotion system. The change from seniority to performance principle in wage and promotion looked like an incomprehensible task for most attendants.

One day, in February of 1991, Mića Jovanović called the author in Berlin asking him to fly to Munich, because two-day lectures were planned for executives of Energoinvest Co. in Sarajevo. Except the author, nobody was available at that time. Mića Jovanović said the author should come first to Munich, from where a car driver from Serbia would take him overnight to Sarajevo. This meant the driver had to drive all night long and the author had to take a sleep on the rear seat of the car. During midnight, the car must have passed through the Slovenian border, where there was a strict pass and customs control. The driver continued the ride through very complicated, mountainous, zigzag roads. It was still very cold. Finally, the car got to the lecture hall of Energoinvest in Sarajevo around 11 o'clock, later than scheduled at 9 o'clock. When the author entered the lecture hall, some hundred awaiting people gave him a big hand, probably for the reason of overcoming all hindrances overnight during the car driving. The author was very much impressed by their enthusiasm and quick learning. The lecture was again on personnel management and personnel appraisal.

The author stayed at Holiday Inn in Sarajevo. In the evening of the first day, he was taken out to the center of old town of Sarajevo. It was a two-day intensive training course for Energoinvest's executives which evoked great attention from attendants, since the subject 'personnel appraisal' was completely unknown to them. The author first explained the personnel appraisal system with concrete examples and then let attendants experiment with that system themselves. They grasped the application of the personnel appraisal very quickly. The system the author used for the lecture here was a slightly modified version of personnel and performance evaluation system of Toyota Motors Plant. No doubt there were many kinds of evaluation systems, however, they were rarely applied to firms in Europe. The author could easily explain this evaluation system and its consequences, as well as disadvantages in use. The author got the feeling that attendants had big fun using the evaluation system for exemplar situation.

Hardly had the author finished his two-day lectures, came a lady coming from Belgrade with Jovanović's assignment. She said that we should leave Sarajevo before it gets dark. We drove to a place looking like a golf place, not a regular airport. There was a small private air plane waiting for us. We started for Belgrade immediately. During the flight to Belgrade, the mentioned lady said to the author that it may be possible that "the war begins soon" (which meant later the Bosnian War). At the airport of Belgrade, Mića Jovanović was waiting for us. He said "you came back safely!" The author felt a bad omen.

In the meantime, the war broke out. About five months later, the author happened to watch TV. Exactly on that day, the Holiday Inn he stayed several months ago was totally bombed down within two seconds, nothing left.

The Bosnian War was over in 1995. Unfortunately, Kosovo conflict started immediately after. The culmination of this was heavy NATO bombings of Serbia and Belgrade in 1999. Chanaron and the author continued to come to Serbia.

During their lectures, NATO bombings took place many times, sometimes very close to the lecture hall. The author could remember the bombing in 1945, when he was very young and American air force bombed down in Pusan. At that time, he was in middle school. Since then, he did not experience bombing anymore. It was really astonishing that bombs fell on civilians and civilian houses.

3. Birth of Megatrend Business School

3.1. Decision in Favor of Zajecar: Decentralisation and "Customers Satisfaction" – Parochialism?

Jovanović's decision to favor Zajecar for his business school was not his parochialism, but hinged on his visionary pragmatic rationality. We will try to go behind the concealed stories. Jovanović took the author many times to the Bor Copper Mining Co. about 30 Km away from Zajecar. He drove first on the highway bound for Greece about 160 km away from Belgrade. Jovanović and the author took this highway more than 20 times for visiting Bor, Zajecar, Nish, and Smederevo. Whenever we were on the highway, the author noticed a relatively little traffic, even though this highway was leading to Greece and Turkey. Probably, the Bosnian crisis and the conflict in Kosovo might have been the cause for little traffic volume.

The first operational basis for Jovanović's project in local towns was the city Bor, because this town was among the 3 biggest copper mines in the world. The copper extracting and processing industry has been known for exporting prefabricated copper raw materials and products, and thus the Government regarded this town as an important post in the region which led to the establishment of the Technical Faculty of Belgrade National University with an emphasis on Mining Engineering. Mića Jovanović's father, Dr. Božin Jovanović used to be head of this Copper Mining Company for 10 years. Since Mića Jovanović was partly grown up in this region, the city Bor was like a hometown for Mića Jovanović.

Mića Jovanović and the author appeared for the first time in mid 80s in a hall on the 2nd floor of a big building belonging to the Bor Copper Mining Company. The hall used as classroom looked grey and gloomy. The first lectures were attended by a group of 50 persons working at top-management of the Bor Copper Mining Company. Mića Jovanović knew everybody.

The author's first lecture translated into Serbian by Mića Jovanović was on the perspective of *'mineral resources versus human resources'*. The first statement by the author was shocking for the Bor Copper Mining Company's executives that mineral resources including copper would be exhaustible in near future. The mineral resources which had played an important role for industrial production would be limited and nature-deteriorating in most cases. The time point would come for a paradigm change accentuating human resources development. Developing, improving and organizing human resources would be more necessary and crucial in future. Stating the 'uselessness of mineral resources in front of the people working in copper mining company' was audacious. But he euphemistically argued that way. Finally, he proposed the name of the town "Bor" to be interpreted as "**B**etter **O**rganizing **R**esources". At the entrance of the town, it was said that since then there was a nameplate of Bor, with a description by Prof. P., Free University Berlin. Later, an Austrian company intended to take over this company, but failed to do so. We do not know why. Then, a Russian company tried it again, and failed as well. Again, we do not know why. The author thought that even a private company with *strategic mineral resources* of great importance for the national economy would be taken over by foreign MNCs in the process of globalization. This is also a big difference between mineral resources and human resources!

He cited from experiences in Japan, Taiwan and Korea which lacked mineral resources, but which have been greatly successful in industrialization by means of utilizing human resources in an effective way.

Nevertheless, Jovanović was successful in bringing EU-supported TEMPUS in 1990s to Bor for the education of engineers which has been greatly supported by Prof. Chanaron.

3.2. Amateurism versus Professionalism

Thanks to the importance of the city BOR's cooper mining for the national economy, the National University of Belgrade had a dependent "Technical Faculty". Its dean was Prof. Zivkovic, former Professor of Civil Engineering at University of Novi Sad. He was a French speaking, very kind and ambitious gentleman. Communication with foreigners was not easy but he managed to get understood by combining of some French and English words. He looked extremely dynamic, and full of temper and persuaded Mića Jovanović to set up a business school in Bor.

At that time, Prof. Zivkovic managed "Business Administration Department" which attempted to combine Engineering and Management under his leadership. Jovanović helped him a great deal by bringing foreign experts to Bor, because he had little contact with foreign scholars of management.

Mr. Zivkovic was successful in establishing a Master course for Business Administration at his Technical Faculty in 1992 with Jovanović's help. The chances to have contacts with foreign experts granted by Mića Jovanović were expected to be conducive to establishing a Business School in Bor. At the beginning, Mića Jovanović also seemed to be attracted by Mr. Zivkovic's dynamism and idea concerning a Business School in Bor. An eventual alliance between Zivkovic and Jovanović might have been possible. However, the procedure of setting up a private business school in Bor took Mića Jovanović too long time due to bureaucratic red tape. In the meantime, Jovanović made decision to choose Zajecar as a site for the future business school. Also the fact that responsible persons in Zajecar were dynamic and quick at decision-making reinforced Jovanović to extent locational preference to Zajecar. Mića Jovanović's decision was to bless Zajecar with the *first* dependence of Megatrend University. To be frank, the author welcomed Jovanović's decision, simply because his intention was to get a private business school established, not a school with a 'semi-private' nature under the auspices of a state university. Additionally, Mića Jovanović would not have had freedom of making all kinds of decisions related to the contents of curriculum.

After the decision was made to get a Business School established in Zajecar, he felt soon that the Business School in Zajecar needed an extra building for his school instead of continuing the lease contract with the city administration and the city hospital. He happened to get an old building offered on the hill of Zajecar. That building was in a bad condition. He purchased that building and renovated it. (see the picture on the next page).

The Bor region is surrounded by beautiful hills, lakes and many small brooks which have been known as a resort for wealthy people and high ranking politicians. In winter, skiing possibilities are given. After hard lectures, sometimes Prof. Chanaron and the author went to a hotel-like pension which was completely covered with snow. It was sometimes very cold and heavy snows blocked traffic. To have a business school in this remote area looked venturesome. However, judging from the current situation of young people's learning motivation in this area, Jovanović's decision was more than correct. The author learned recently that responsible persons of the city administration and the Bor Copper Mining Co. would repent of having lost a 'big fish' (Business School). Some years ago he went to Zajecar with Prof. Wolfgang Jahnke in order to give some lectures on the economics of lifestyle and met Prof. Zivkovic as an attendant there. The author asked him what he was doing at that moment. His answer was very short: " I am now an employee of Mića".

Megatrend Business School in Zajecar

The author's first visit to Zajecar was very exciting. About 30 km away from Bor, the road to Zajecar was in a disastrous condition. Obviously, the town Zajecar, without any noteworthy industry and a small border shared with Bulgaria was not so attractive for the national economy compared to Bor. But Zajecar was famous for legacies of the Roman Empire called

Felix Romuliana which was located only 10 kilometers west of Zajecar. Roman Emperor Gaius Valerius was born, lived and died in Felix Romuliana. He recognized Christianity in 311 A.D., two years before famous "Milan Edict". The city is, also, well known for having brought up many famous personalities in politics, economy, culture and sports such as Nikola Pasic (famous prime minister of Serbia in the beginning of XX century), Svetozar Markovic (philosopher), Zoran Radmilovic (one of the greatest actors of all time of Serbia), Dr. Božin Jovanović (famous partisan's commander in the World War II and great politician after the war), etc. Not to forget is the famous patriot Veljko Petrovic who organized the first uprising against Ottoman Turks in early XIX century.

This region reminded the author very much of those two places he worked at: the *one* is the Northeast Region ("*pa-isan*" in Thai implying 'backwardness') of Thailand, where he worked in 1966 in connection with the Mekong River Regional Development. This area bordering Laos and Cambodia had a great difficulty with flood nearly every year. Two dams *Nampoong* and *Nampong* were constructed on the Thai side. Since then, the regional development based on agriculture-centered community development (*patna chumchon*) was expected to be embarked on. The task of the author was to persuade local elites to join the regional development. Interestingly, the Thai government made a decision to set up a new university at Konkaen which became now one of the best universities in Thailand. The author learned that this university recognized the major role of bringing up local business and development managers for Northeast of Thailand; The *other* one is the region Yanji, triangle region between China, North Korea and Soviet Union habituated by the Korean minority, distant from the central region of China. This minority has been known to be poor and backward, lacking earning possibilities. Young people sought new job opportunities but they lacked skills and qualifications. Under this condition, a private university called 'Yanbian University of Science and Technology' was established 20 years ago, with engineering, computer sciences, nursing science, management, etc. This university asked the author to help implement its internationalization. The author had helped the university as vice-president for 7 years. Fortunately, this university is now aligning with best higher education institutions in China.

To sum up, the remote, forgotten and poor region can develop and create its own venture-identity by means of a new type of university, as we have experienced in Israel (Ben Gurion University), Thailand (Kon Kaen University), China (Yanbian University of Science and Technology), Korea (POSTEC), etc. What is needed for this undertaking is courage to deal first with human resources.

It was very understandable for Mića Jovanović to try to make a substantial contribution to his hometown by establishing a business school. Once he also had a plan to set up the school on the ruins of Felix Romuliana (IV century A.D.) "Felix Romuliana Management School", but he gave it up later, because this cultural site is in possession of the city administration of Zajecar. (see the picture below).

Felix Romuliana, IV century A.D. The Palace of the Roman Emperor Gaius Valerius.

Mića Jovanović took many foreign scholars such as Prof. Stockwin (Oxford), Dr. Amstutz (Harvard), Prof. Jahnke (Berlin) etc., to Zajecar. These professors were happy to be in Zajecar, otherwise they could not have had a chance to see the Serbian countryside, they said. These people were visiting many countries in the world for lecturing, but had a little chance to get in touch with local culture and people in the rural area. They said *unisono*, especially the Balkan region is full of colorful diversity of races, ethnicities, religions and nationalities which may be suggestive of the upcoming future of humankind in the process of globalization.

The author was once taken to the main auditorium of the Zajecar City Hospital and also to the main auditorium of the Zajecar City Administration. Both halls were not used except for some special festivities. Mića Jovanović's idea was to rent these spaces for lectures of his school at the beginning stage. He entered into agreement with the city hospital and the city administration for a long-term lease. Mića Jovanović's friends were impressed with this idea to *begin with lectures first in unused local public halls.*

Author at his first lecturing in Zajecar, 1995.

3.2.1. Win-Win-Win Situation:

The author's first lecture to local students in Zajecar was held in the big hall of the city hospital, of which the capacity could house more than 1000 persons. But his lecture was attended by only 50 students. The other day, more students came. He heard from other colleagues who gave lecture in the main auditorium of the city administration that they were really impressed by enthusiasm and concentration of students.

Most lecturers confirmed *unisono* that to run a business school in the way as envisaged by Mića Jovanović was a *win-win-win situation*:

First, local students do not need to go to urban regions such as Belgrade, so that they can stay at home with their parents (*cost saving effect*).

Megatrend Business School in Zajecar, 1995.

Professor Jovanović and the author, Zajecar, 1995.

Second, local administration/hospital can earn revenue for leasing lecture halls instead of keeping their spaces unused (*earning effect*),

Third, Mića Jovanović can contribute to the local development in the sense that young people are able to join local events and daily life (*participation effect).*

It was very plausible that the Megatrend Business School was awarded a Special Prize for Contribution to Local Development by the Zajecar City Administration. Here, a new model of higher education institution is being probed in the sense that "teaching staff go to students, not students to teachinq staff". This is a sort of new *'customers satisfaction'*!

The development of higher education and urbanization are said to have a close interrelationship. With the progress of urbanization, rural people rush into urban areas. The increasing population conducive to urbanization has to provide different services, such as education, medical service etc. Young people leave rural areas for urbanized cities for higher education. The result of this process is that rural areas are hollowed from young people, whilst the aged people are left in the rural region, increasing the impoverishment. Advanced countries are mostly faced with sharpening of this urban-rural gap. So to speak, Mića Jovanović brought a new message of fighting against this gap by means of establishment of a new school. This effort resulted in a success that many young people stopped moving out of Zajecar and enjoyed higher education in their hometown.

The practice by Mića Jovanović to utilize unused local public halls for lectures which successfully started in Zajecar was later applied to other towns such as Pozarevac, Backa Topola, Valjevo, Vrsac, Jagodina, etc. This effort entailed reactivation of idle facilities and infrastructures with a large *re-cyling effect.*

3.2.2. Modularization of Study Programs:

The other interesting experiment which was systematically institutionalized is *modularization of study programs.* All detachments are being served by *mobile university mini-bus* bringing a group of professors from Belgrade, or better to say, rotating professors. For instance, a certain week is reserved for *international economy and management lectures.* During this very week,

Author at his lecturing in Zajecar, 2012.

Aerial photo of Megatrend Business School in Zajecar, 2012.

only those directly related lectures such as international finance, organizations, banking, FDI, international insurance, international distribution, etc. are given. This *rotation-supported modular system* was unique and has been greatly lauded by EU. This epoch-making reform, introduction of modular system, which has been experimented in many European countries but in vain, implemented in Serbia with Megatrend University showed a great success.

This system bears following advantages:

- first, *cost-saving aspect*: each detachment in Serbian local towns cannot employ and keep so many professors and teaching staff for themselves. Here, the sharing of a group of teaching staff by all detachments was made possible;
- second, *continuation of direct communication between professors and students* is possible during the whole week. The traditional way of teaching offers professors communication with students only once a week for a short time. Through the one-week intensive communication, much more learning motivation of students can be expected;
- third, *students stay at home* participating in all kinds of daily local life and family work, and also evoking many kinds of cultural and social activities at local level.

The decentralization policy was supported by the university-owned TV Metropolis station by means of disseminating special lectures and special events nationwide.

A propos TV station, one can stress its supplementary function for lectures held in Belgrade. In case a renowned expert with very busy schedule is not able to stay longer than one day, he can deliver his special lecture on TV. For instance, this happened with the alternative peace Nobel Prize awardee Johan Galtung. Or in other cases, Profs. Stockwin (Oxford), Dr. Amstutz (Harvard), the author (Berlin) and Jovanović (Megatrend) held a roundtable discussion on the future of higher education in Serbia at Metropolis TV station in Belgrade. All Megatrend detachments were connected *live* during the discussion.

Johan Galtung

Zajecar as a small town adjacent to the Bulgarian and Romanian borders affects the life of the city, a variety of small traditional handicraft shops and also shops involved in border trade which makes this town colorful and multi-racial. It has been often said that "the people of Zajecar is akin to the mentality and culture of Vidin, Bulgaria and Timosoara, Romania." This is also the reason why students from Bulgaria and Romania were enrolled at the Zajecar which strengthened cooperation between Zajecar Business School and University in Sofia, Bulgaria and University of Timosoara, Romania.

Agriculture is dominant. Only a very small part of population is living on handicraft and horse-raising. There are nearly nothing as noteworthy as sightseeing sites. Therefore, in former time the move of young people to the region of Belgrade was very common. Without Megatrend Business School, many young people might have left for Belgrade. Probably it may be certain that this area could have been hollowed from young people. Interesting is the fact that the population has been increasing since some years, especially the proportion of young people which may be thanks to studying possibility at Megatrend University. Now the population of Zajecar Municipality counts more than 60.000.

The people in Zajecar were very thankful to Mića Jovanović that many prominent scholars visited there to give lectures, such as Prof. Arthur Stockwin, Oxford University (on the role of Japanese economy in the world economy), Prof Wolfgang Jahnke, Berlin University of Applied Sciences (Creativity and Venture Business), Prof. Abo Tetsuo, Tokyo University (Globalization of Production System), etc. Megatrend University here rounded up many educational institutions in the city such as Technical School, Medical School, Nursing School, etc.

To bring these prominent professors to Zajecar was not simple. It was not the question of honorarium. Mića Jovanović was not able to offer high honorarium deserved for those professors. Rather, these scholars were from the beginning impressed with the idea of Mića Jovanović to disseminate modern capitalistic market economy into the rural area and to contribute to rural development. Still, a question remains whether it is possible to get a comprehensive business school established in this triangle covering students from three countries, eventually in the *future campus of Felix Romuliana*.

Map of detachments of Megatrend University.
(Red points show all the cities in Serbia where Megatrend University had and still has its schools)

Graduate School of Biofarming, Backa Topola, 2012.

Students of Graduate School of Biofarming on practical lessons in greenhouse, 2012.

3.3. Lean Management, Group Work and TQC in Smederevo

The biggest steel plant of Serbia MKS (later SARTID), located in Smederevo on the way from Zajecar to Belgrade, organized a seminar at the beginning of 1990s. This city with about 90.000 inhabitants with a big port at the Danube River was important for the Serbian economy. Mića Jovanović, Dr. Martine Bercovici (CNRS) from France and the author were invited to give talks on Lean Management and work organization at the shop level.

Jovanović and the author knew that the Lean Management which was the world-wide popular management technique at that time would be new for Serbia, probably for two reasons: first, most companies in Serbia were under self-management principle in socialist economy; second, the management- and economics-related academic world of Serbia was so long isolated from the outward world that Serbian scholars and experts had no chance to get familiar with new expertise from the West. As a matter of fact, the 1980s and 1990s in Western management science and practice were a decisive period, in which the Western management system and techniques were faced with the challenges of Japanese Toyota production system and techniques. Serbia had not been affected by this new development of management science and practice. Mića Jovanović and Megatrend University undertook efforts for the first time in Serbia to introduce the Lean Management, Group Work, Kaizen, Just-In-Time, Supply Chain Management, etc.

At Smederevo company, the author's contribution focused on group work and quality control management in Japan, Korea and Germany. Instead of *statistical quality control* which has been popular in the West, he emphasized *individual quality control* by means of QC circles, system quality control and Total Quality Control (TQC).

In European companies, the concept of 'quality' has been understood as a *mechanical* one which was in practice associated with the use of statistical methods. Also, despite the so-called 'quality inspection system', most products and firms have been suffering from insufficiency in quality control. The new concept the author introduced was the so-called TQC which hinged on the totality of workers' spirit. The quality was interrelated with price and time, as the following picture indicates, embodied in a trinity of Total Cost Control (TCC) and Total Delivery (time) Control (TDC). In practical implementation of TQC, the most important part is that the top-management understands its philosophy and logic, and begin with putting it into practice, so that the workforce can internalize the quality in connection with cost and delivery (time).

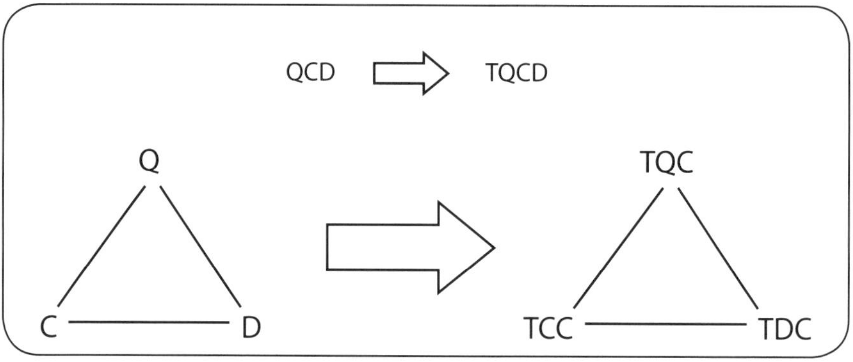

The author stressed that the lean management is also strongly related to the continuous change of workers' spirit, even though the lean production is interpreted as cost reduction strategy in the West. This means that the change of workers' consciousness and spirit toward the increase of efficiency is the pre-condition for the lean production, as the following picture by Ohno Taiichi shows.

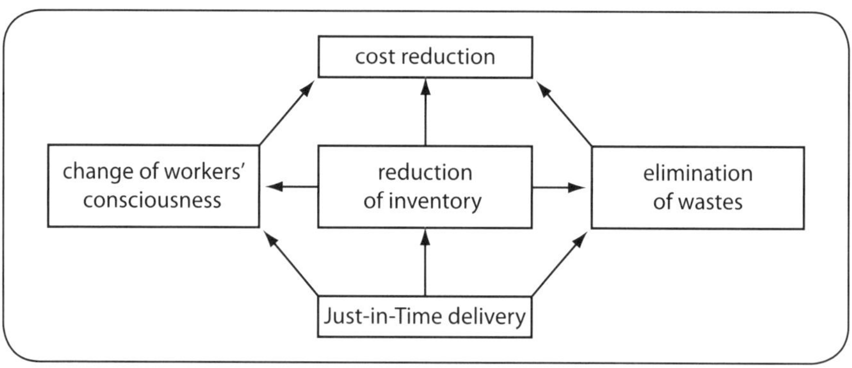

Further, he gave also some detailed information about the practice of Volkswagen, because as advisor for Volkswagen, he had an assignment to train Chinese workforce to get familiar with the Just-in-Time principle in subcontracted Shanghai Volkswagen Plant and its Supply Chain Management in the 1980s. In the process of transformation in China, the most serious problem was to change workers' morale and spirit.

The author thought this experience could be applied to Serbia to a certain degree. He further stressed: for a shift from self-management to capitalistic lean management, it was absolutely necessary to define connotation of a work group and a new incentive system for the work groups. In socialist economy and self-management economy, the group was not autonomous and was *forcibly formed* neglecting incentives and learning effect. Experiences with practice of group work in East Germany were that most workers were extremely hesitant about the use of group work, because they have been accustomed to working in groups (Arbeitskampfgruppen) for a long time.

The president of MKS (Mr. Rade Colic) who had served as representative of Serbian Trade Organization in New York, was very receptive toward Western management techniques and was present while the seminar was ongoing. His question was pinpointing as regards how to introduce group work. He was afraid that the new group work system could be easily understood as a counter-concept of self-management. For solving eventual discrepancies between lean group work system and self-management system, the author referred to the importance of group leadership that should be capable of persuading and leading the workforce.

Dr. Bercovici experienced in her anthropological study on French car plants pointed out the difficulty at the beginning stage of introduction of lean group work system in France and the necessity of intensive training and communication of top-managers. A serious problem in France was that shop-floors were strongly influenced by radical left-wing oriented unions. For neutralizing these radical influences, new material incentives were very instrumental.

As regards intra-company communication, the president of that company wanted to know whether Fayol's model could be applied to his organization. Jovanović and the author pointed to necessity of classifying the communication at least into two categories: first, interdepartmental and interdivisional communication; and second, the communication at shop-level. Communication in the latter case does not need any additional organizational 'trick', but new arrangement of incentives for workers at shop-level, such as bonus, overtime payment, prolongation of legal holidays etc. However, to change the spirit and morale of workers in connection with new group work, system has to be pursued gradually. As far as the communication among departments and divisions is concerned, one cannot neglect the persistent sticking by top-management to the "line organization" principle which has existed for many decades. The president said that he would not be able to introduce any kind of *additional compulsory rules* which could give birth to new labor conflicts in the company. Further he said: When the first transformation wave arrived with a message of introducing "group work" (leaning on Japanese shop floor system), it was hard for the top-management to persuade shop-floor leaders who were very concerned about eventual disappearance of self-management. "We must study psychology of Serbian workers first of all", he added. Mića Jovanović claimed that there is a great shortage of study on work psychology disclosing practice of companies' daily work situation.

3.4. Official Opening of Megatrend Business School: The First Business School in Southeast Europe

The day of Dec. 27, 1989 is marking the official opening of Megatrend Business School. As it was already shown, many kinds of preparations were successfully accomplished. Thus, the official opening of the Megatrend Business School seemed to be only the question of time.

To summarize preparations:

- securing of sourcing teaching persons from renowned institutions and universities abroad subsumed under 'global talent pool'
- accession to most modern Western management and business studies ('knowledge-based infrastructure') by means of membership in Euro-Asia Management Studies Association and Global University Network (NEWS)
- decentralization of knowledge and infrastructural, legal, and organizational basis ('go to customers') by means of establishing local detachments.

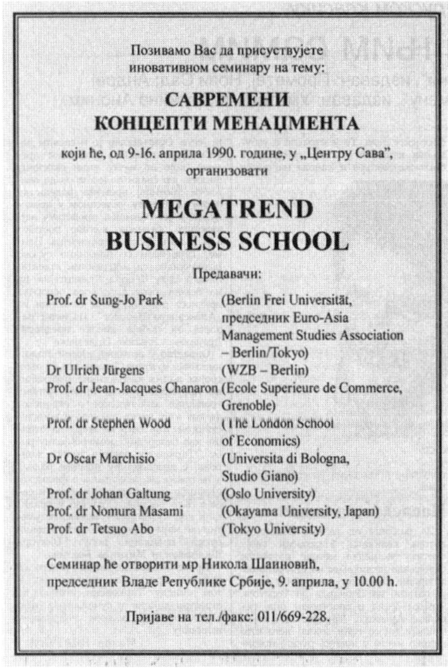

Позивамо Вас да присуствујете иновативном семинару на тему:

САВРЕМЕНИ КОНЦЕПТИ МЕНАЏМЕНТА

који ће, од 9-16. априла 1990. године, у „Центру Сава", организовати

MEGATREND BUSINESS SCHOOL

Предавачи:

Prof. dr Sung-Jo Park	(Berlin Frei Universität, председник Euro-Asia Management Studies Association – Berlin/Tokyo)
Dr Ulrich Jürgens	(WZB – Berlin)
Prof. dr Jean-Jacques Chanaron	(Ecole Superieure de Commerce, Grenoble)
Prof. dr Stephen Wood	(The London School of Economics)
Dr Oscar Marchisio	(Universita di Bologna, Studio Giano)
Prof. dr Johan Galtung	(Oslo University)
Prof. dr Nomura Masami	(Okayama University, Japan)
Prof. dr Tetsuo Abo	(Tokyo University)

Семинар ће отворити мр Никола Шаиновић, председник Владе Републике Србије, 9. априла, у 10.00 h.

Пријаве на тел./факс: 011/669-228.

Announcement for the first seminar of the Megatrend Business School, April 1990.

As regards buildings and facilities for the new school, the first decision was to rent old buildings located scattered in downtown of Belgrade. Classrooms lacking modern teaching facilities and technical equipment were renewed. This was the same in case of local detachments. (see the following list of local detachments)

The first seminar for 105 general managers from former Socialistic Federal Republic of Yugoslavia, held in April 1990.

List of all Megatrend Schools:

- GRADUATE SCHOOL OF BUSINESS STUDIES - BELGRADE
- GRADUATE SCHOOL OF CULTURE AND MEDIA - BELGRADE
- GRADUATE SCHOOL OF INTERNATIONAL ECONOMY - BELGRADE
- GRADUATE SCHOOL OF STATE AND PUBLIC ADMINISTRATION - BELGRADE
- GRADUATE SCHOOL OF ART AND DESIGN - BELGRADE
- GRADUATE SCHOOL OF BIOFARMING – BACKA TOPOLA
- COLLEGE OF BIOFARMING – BACKA TOPOLA
- GRADUATE SCHOOL OF MANAGEMENT - ZAJECAR
- GRADUATE SCHOOL OF BUSINESS ECONOMY - VALJEVO
- GRADUATE SCHOOL OF BUSINESS STUDIES - POZAREVAC
- GRADUATE SCHOOL OF COMPUTER SCIENCES - BELGRADE
- GRADUATE SCHOOL OF BUSINESS STUDIES - VRSAC
- BUSINESS COLLEGE - ZAJECAR
- MEGATREND VIRTUAL UNIVERSITY (DISTANCE LEARNING) - BELGRADE
- INSTITUTE OF NEW TECHNOLOGY – BELGRADE.

Mića Jovanović's strategy was of *Schumacher's credo "small is beautiful"*. Didn't Alvin Tofler say, *"you've got to think about "big things" while you're doing small things, so that all the small things go in the right direction"*?

His first choice out of academic disciplines was management science which does not necessitate huge investment, like engineering, medicine and other natural disciplines, but absolutely necessary at the *first* stage of transformation. Better to say, development of human resources who are to initiate and push ahead development process in conjunction with providing young people with spirit of rationality. This had to be pursued not only in urban Belgrade area, but was to affect local regions. At the *second* stage, one could add computer science, law and public administration, agriculture, and lastly lifestyle-centered disciplines such as arts, design and cultures, media, sports and interculturality-centered geo-economics.

In connection with opening of Megatrend Business School in Belgrade, there were some interesting stories. One of these stories was related to competition among various private business schools in Southeast Europe, for instance in Croatia, Slovenia and Serbia. The reputation enjoyed by Mića Jovanović's university in academic insider circle abroad was that Megatrend University was seen as the *first* business school in the region which affords eligibility of being a good business school, especially because renowned scholars from the USA, Europe and Japan committed themselves to assisting Jovanović's project.

The following story was symptomatic of this background. At the end of 1980s there was an international experts meeting organized by EAMSA (Euro-Asia Management Studies Association) and INSEAD in Fontainebleau dealing with intercultural management in former socialist economies. Prof. Helmut Schuette affiliated with INSEAD introduced to the audience a woman from Slovenia (Mrs. Danica Purg) as a scholar who was believed to succeed in setting up a Western type business school in the region of Southeast Europe. Then she stated with pride " I established the first business school with help of Prof. Schuette in the region of Southeast Europe". However, in fact, Megatrend Business School had already been existed for several years.

At least more than 5 attendants such as Profs. Ikeda, Abo, (Japan), Juergens and Park (Germany), Hernadi (Hungary) etc. said very loudly "This is not true! We have already been many times in Belgrade giving lectures at Megatrend Business School". The question was, in fact, not relevant, which school when was established. At that time noteworthy was a certain competition among former socialist economies as regards who is forerunner in introducing and spreading Western management theories and techniques. It was interesting that some established well-known business schools in Europe took the position that new schools in former socialist economies were to rely on already known schools. This meant a new business school in a former socialist economy was supposed to be a sort of *branch school'* of the already established university. There were pro-and-contra discussions which way would be better either to rely on what an established business school 'grants', or to get a new business school established by means of independent efforts. To be short, some experts of established schools were likely to think in a biased way that only this kind of 'branch school' is a real one. In contrast, the approach by Mića Jovanović was absolutely different from the 'branch school' approach in the sense that he initiated such a project that foreign and domestic colleagues came together to push ahead a new university.

The host of the above-mentioned meeting was Prof. Helmut Schuette, affiliated with INSEAD, who was not hesitant to favor Slovenia as regards the establishment of business school. In this occasion, he said to the author: "The President of EAMSA (at that time the author was President of EAMSA) should accompany the newly opened Business School in Slovenia". He replied, "I am ready to help them, not as President, but as an individual person, if people ask me for help".

Some business schools emerged in Serbia, such as Metropolitan University, Alpha University, Singidunum University, European University, etc. Compared to all these schools, Megatrend University had a competitive advantage as regards international networking, global experts pool, globalization of university dependences, local detachments of university in Serbia, modularization of curriculum, virtual university, etc., to name only some.

The naming of universities in Serbia is interesting. Most of them have a reference to the Serbian history and the region Europe which is to symbolize 'something particular'.

The typical case of this is Singidunum and European University. As far as Megatrend University is concerned, it was solely Jovanović's choice. He probably sought in this entitlement the vision to go to future like Megatrend.

It goes without mentioning that Megatrend Business School was an impeccably successful project serving as a pioneer in Southeast Europe as regards introduction of Western management principles and techniques. However, beyond the fact that at least a decade-long intensive preparations were done in all respects, one should mention that now Megatrend University, with more than 600 professors and many foreign adjunct professors, can be proud of immeasurable education skill accumulation and university-industry cooperation, playing a key role in pursuing the knowledge economy of Serbia. Nevertheless, the question remains how the quality and reputation of teaching staff can keep pace with their colleagues in the West and Asia. The author is of opinion that, regardless of any comment on teaching staff of Megatrend University, the increasing global network would bring more progress in the future.

3.5. Samsung and Megatrend University

Mića Jovanović paid a visit to Seoul in 1997. He went to Korea with the vice-president of the Federal Republic of Yugoslavia (Mr. Vladan Kutlesic) in order to attend the World Political Science Congress. However, his intention was to make a promotion for his university in Korea. The author, while staying as visiting professor at Seoul National University, had time to accompany him and to make schedules during his sojourn. He paid a courtesy visit to Seoul National University in order to talk about cooperation possibilities with Megatrend University and its Graduate School of Business Studies.

Very important was one of his schedule giving an interview to the Samsung-affiliated newspaper "Choongang Daily" which already knew Jovanović's visit. Since at that time Samsung was greatly interested to accede to the Balkan market, it wanted to know what would be happening in Serbia. On this occasion, Jovanović gave an interview which was printed in the 'Choongang Ilbo' of August 26, 1997, as follows. (the Korean-written interview see the appendix II)

Choongang Daily: *You already visited Korea some years ago. What is your impression about Seoul?*

Jovanović: I notice many high buildings and cars running in Seoul. What is striking is that common people on the street look very bright and sophisticated, and their expressions are dynamic.

Choongang Daily: *We know that you got your Ph.D. from LSE and had experiences to teach at Universities in London. You are a famous scholar in business administration in Eastern Europe and established a business school. Please tell us about your school.*

Jovanović: I set up the business school in 1989 and we have now 3700 students. I am sure that our school is for the time-being the best one, even though the history is not so long. Students are very ambitious to learn in order to contribute to system transformation.

Choongang Daily: *You have served as advisor for the automobile plant Zastava in Serbia. We know that you are very much interested in the Korean car industry.*

Jovanović: Yes, the Zastava plant exported 0.2 million cars to the USA. After the collapse of the Socialist Federal Republic of Yugoslavia, the production volume diminished to 10.000 units. The plant is now in a great difficulty waiting for a takeover by a foreign company. Korea was successful in establishing an autonomous auto industry without relying on foreign countries. If a Korean company would take over Zastava that will become an interesting cooperation model. Unfortunately, Serbia is exposed to UN sanctions due to the Bosnian Crisis. Nevertheless, the inflation rate amounted to 4.5% despite the mentioned sanctions, and the exchange rate in last three years was stable. Serbia is among the countries with the highest income level and strongest economic potential compared to all former communist countries.

Choongang Daily: *Thanks.*

During his sojourn, the Center of Samsung Corporation called "chairman's secretariat" (*bisu-shil*) assigned an executive Dr. Kim Wanpyo (Department of Strategic Management, Samsung) to take care of Mića Jovanović regarding all kinds of events. Jovanović and Dr. Kim had known each other since the 12th EAMSA conference at Bocconi University in Milano (1995). Thus, it was possible for Jovanović to visit the plant of Samsung Electronics Co. in Suwon near Seoul. After a very friendly reception extended to Mića Jovanović, he was asked to provide qualified graduates for Samsung.

As regards the relation between Megatrend University and Samsung, the representative of Samsung in Belgrade was very proud of his son who was already studying at Megatrend University and took time to join the inauguration ceremony for the first president (the author) of Megatrend University. The Seoul Headquarters of Samsung assigned him to attend that ceremony, since the author used to serve Samsung Motors Co. as advisor for a long time.

Then Mića Jovanović, Ana Langovic and the author visited the Samsung Branch Co. in Belgrade in order to seek cooperation possibilities with Megatrend University. The Samsung CEO in Belgrade had shown great interest in creating an internship program for students of Megatrend University. Actually, Megatrend University and Samsung are location-wise neighbors in the new town of Belgrade which made close dialogue possible. After materializing the project "Korea Center" of Megatrend University, the cooperation between them will bear very fruitful outcome.

4. Transformation Determinants

The author of this book would like to present 3 interviews in the following. These interviews are with Dr. Božin Jovanović, Prof. Mića Jovanović and Prof. J. J. Chanaron, all of whom have been heavily involved in creation and development of the project Megatrend from the beginning on, and offer an interesting overview on philosophy, strategy, and trajectories of Megatrend University.

4.1. Conceptual Perception 1: Interview with Dr. Božin Jovanović, January 26, 2011.

Dr. Božin Jovanović (1920-2011)

Dr. Božin Jovanović is father of Prof. Mića Jovanović and was known to be a mentor for Megatrend University. He died a bit more than 3 months after this interview.

The interviewer (the author): *I know that you have played an important role when deciding on the future course of Megatrend University at many decisive moments, and that rector, professor Jovanović, has always turned to you for advice. Can you mention some important points in the history of the university which you consider to be crucial?*

Božin Jovanović: A long time ago, when Mića organized a three-day seminar in the Sava Centre for the managers of the largest Yugoslav companies of the Socialist Federal Republic of Yugoslavia, when there were 105 general managers from all republics, when the seminar was opened by the Prime Minister, and when Mića gave the opening speech, I saw that he had certain inclinations to education, that he had some abilities to organize that work and deal with it. That moment with 105 general managers from all over Yugoslavia listening to foreign lecturers, that moment, both for me and Mića, was not so much a turning point, but rather another confirmation that we should focus on the development of education in Serbia, i.e. Yugoslavia.

The interviewer: *This turned out to be the right direction. And now, what do you think about this phase, when university is already more than twenty years old, in which direction should the university go at this phase?*

Božin Jovanović: I suggested to Mića not to widen up the university any more, except in specific cases, but to focus on enhancing the quality of lectures, text books, exams, relation with the students, etc., the fight for quality in its widest sense. If we want this to become really 'the right education', as he put it, than there must be an organized, deliberate struggle for the quality of lectures, exams, the relations with students, etc. Some new schools could be opened only under specific circumstances, but basically it shouldn't be done, since 12 faculties, 4 colleges, an institute, and more than 25000 thousand students are more than enough. Wouldn't you agree?

The interviewer: *You kept saying that success should be measured not only by the number of graduate students, but also by the number of students who got employed.*

Božin Jovanović: You are right. That is what I keep saying to Mića and those in charge of the faculty in Kraljevica (Zajecar). Daily records must be kept on the employment, especially of those who graduated, got their master's and Ph.D. degrees. The rate of employment shows the results of our work. What those people have accomplished in their companies determines the quality of our work. We must create experts who, when they enter economy, i.e. an organization, an institution, will be able to become fully integrated in the shortest time and achieve results that will justify the investments in their education.

The interviewer: *That should be so as a rule, although our records on employment...*

Božin Jovanović: You are right. The person in charge of the coordination centre in Paracin complains that it is difficult to keep records on whether the 20 graduate students from Paracin got a job or not. I believe that it would take me 15 minutes for this task daily. It wouldn't take me more; since there aren't 12 000 of the employed, but only 12.

The interviewer: *But generally speaking, the employment rate here is not very high. We do not keep the record...regarding employment.*

Božin Jovanović: Unfortunately, you are right. But luckily, the smallest number of the unemployed comes from Megatrend. That elementary record we do have. We usually take and analyze the case of Zajecar, and then we generalize this to other centers. And our economy in Serbia (since I am very well informed, for instance, what is happening in Eastern Serbia) is crying for experts, it desperately needs the people who will pull it out from this poverty, hopelessness... This can only be done with the help of the young, educated, responsible people, and they are created by Megatrend. I said that we are the champions in tennis and unemployment. The unemployment rate will be 29%. This is a record, we are the leaders in Europe.

4.2. Conceptual Perception 2

A special interview was arranged with Prof. Mića Jovanović on January 26, 2011. The interview focused on the following three questions.

The author: *Looking back at the last two decades, what was the most serious and difficult impediments for Megatrend University?*

Prof. Jovanović: I will put it in very simple terms. The first impediment was the *beginning* of the undertaking. Since we did not have persons and organizations experienced in handling private university, I had a difficulty to find persons eligible to give proper advices. Thus, I called many experts from abroad. I thought of Schumpeter's theory of 'creative destruction'.

The second was many institutional, organizational and legal barriers. Further, to be more concrete, people were afraid of birth of a mass of private business schools which could entail complicated order of educational market and orientationlessness of young people. I had to persuade these people and institutions.

The author: *What was most important to you?*

Prof. Jovanović: I saw the most important things for transformation of the socialist economy are three: *spirit, people and completely new ideas and concepts*. Since I have enjoyed my training and education abroad and written a book on 'socialistic self-management', it was clear to me that we have to begin anew. That is the reason why I tried to collect renowned excellent scholars and experts around me. These people brought really new expertise and concepts of management which the Serbian economy needs. I was lucky and could succeed in bringing really famous experts from famous universities and companies."

The author: *What is your plan for next two decades?*

Prof. Jovanović: Efficient internationalization and globalization of Megatrend University.

We cite the interview with Prof. Jovanović which was carried out by World Investment News, as follows.

4.3 CONCEPTUAL PERCEPTION 3:

World Investment News Interview with Mića Jovanović, Rector, Megatrend University, Belgrade, 22-06-2010.

Founded in 1989, the Megatrend University is the most prestigious private university of Serbia. Can you tell me the idea of creating the university and the evolution during these 21 years?

In the beginning of the 1980s, after graduating in Belgrade, I went to London to do my Ph.D. at the London School of Economics. After 3 years, I achieved my Ph.D. in the field of industrial relations and successfully defended my thesis. I started teaching on self-management in two institutions: Bradford University and Portsmouth Polytechnics. I already had an idea of setting my own company: Megatrend International Expert Consortium Limited. The purpose of the firm was to give consultancy services to different companies mostly in the automotive industry. On that time, I was included in a huge project of the Massachusetts Institute of Technology (MIT) regarding the future of the work in the automotive industry with the view to developing a very high level of robotization of working process in this field. As you know, at that time and ever since, the automotive industry is the most important industry in the world, side by side with electronics. I spent 5 years doing research in almost all the important car factories in the world from American, South Korean, Japanese and Italian carmakers. I did not have experience with French firms. But my good friend and expert Jean-Jacques Chanaron has worked with French automotive firms and he has been during 2 mandates the President of the Megatrend University before the arrival in April of the new President Walter Schwimmer, former Secretary General of European Council for many years. Mr. Chanaron is still collaborating with Megatrend as a person responsible for the Internationalization of Megatrend University.

Is this connected with the creation of the West London Business School by Megatrend?

Yes, we established West London Business School in December 2009. We have all the licenses and we are still waiting for the accreditation. In fact, we do not need the accreditation because it is a part of Megatrend University, and Megatrend has American and European accreditations. We are fully recognized by every institution and we even have the AQA (American Quality Asociation) and Eduniversal accreditation which ranked us among the first 500 universities of the world.

It is a big recognition for a University that has 21 years.

We entered the 21 years with a huge ceremony in 27th of December 2009. Although it was Christmas period, 17 rectors from whole Europe, full diplomatic representation, 2/3 of Serbian Government and around 700 people from the whole World attended this anniversary.

The presence of 17 rectors of international universities is remarkable. Is international cooperation one of the pillars of Megatrend University?

From the very beginning, we started with the international cooperation. The project with the MIT was the trigger for making this possible to visit automotive plants such as Nissan in Japan or the FIAT factory in Montecasino, and get in contact with universities abroad. All of them supported the idea of creating the first private university in the former Yugoslavia. We actually have 16 campuses and 26.000 students.

What is the mission of the Megatrend University?

When I decided to create the university in the late 1980s I had the idea to make the best university, kind of Harvard University, but in Serbia. I came back from England in 1989 just in time to see the self- management law change. Until 1989, there was a socialist self- management system and therefore, private initiative was strictly forbidden. The first Company Act, which gave the chance to everyone to start own private initiative was adopted in the Federal Parliament in November 1989 and Megatrend was created in December. The only thing I knew how to do was managing university and I invested the money I earned working for 6 years in London as broker of copper futures and options at LME (London Metal Exchange), while I was doing my scientific activities. It was not easy but with a lot of effort and beating lot of obstacles, we made it happen. The most encouraging thing was to receive the support of my colleagues from England, South Korea, Japan and other countries, in creating a quality university.

What makes Megatrend University special compared to other universities?

We have 4 crucial pillars. The first one is having excellent educational programmes; the second is having excellent professors; the third is that we are publishing excellent textbooks with our own printing facilities; and our fourth pillar is our real international cooperation.

We have many agreements with French schools such as Grenoble Ecole de Management and CERAM that includes permanent exchanging of our professors and students. We have franchised our economic programs with the Management School of Grenoble for the Master of International Business (MIB) and for the Bachelor of International Business (BIB). The school in Grenoble announced us 3 years ago as the best partner, having in mind that they have 60 or 65 partners all over the world.

Is it the same agreement that you have with the Spanish University and Research Center Ortega y Gasset?

Yes, it is. The Vice Rector for International Relations, Professor Pajovic, signed the contract and I think that I will go in September to Spain to start officially. Moreover, we have excellent relations with the Berlin Freie Universitaet, with Italians universities like the Mediterranean University from Bari and the University from Naples.

What are the future challenges of the Megatrend University?

Actually the virtual university is our fifth pillar and is the only one in South-East Europe. We have more than 90 books that include our software codes. Our virtual university is the creation of a mathematical genius, our professor Veliko Spasic, who won an international award in 2002 in San Francisco. He made it according to my ideas.

One more curiosity about us: Megatrend University had the first website in the history of this part of Europe. It was in 1994. Regarding the development of IT sector we have many advantages because we have an excellent school of mathematics and creative people, and the mathematics is the crucial base for the computer sciences.

Minister of Education Mr. Zarko Obradovic mentioned us about the large number of awards that Serbian students are receiving in sciences.

Yes, not only students from universities but from the high schools as well. In the last 5 years, in the mathematics Olympic Games, Serbia won every one out of three medals, either golden, silver or bronze ones. We do have an excellent line of education in the field of mathematics. We have our own school for computer sciences with a famous mathematician Dean, Professor Grada Milovanovic. He is considered to be among the top 3 mathematicians of the world.

Is Megatrend taking part in the Bologna process?

I am strongly against Bologna and I have been fighting against for more than 5 years. There are several reasons: first of all, the concept of study is not very good. There is not enough interactive communication between professor and the students. Bologna's concept of education is killing creativity by using test exams. Moreover, it is too expensive and the output of this education is too low for the cost. For instance, if we respect Bologna process in Belgrade, there should be 4 m^2 for each of students. Our ratio is 1^2 for student because we have a bit more than 25.000 m^2 of space for 26000 students, which proved to be more than sufficient for education purposes. We did not have 26.000 students all the time.

There are many countries that are going to give up Bologna such as France, Germany, United Kingdom and Slovenia. Even in Serbia, I am convincing people not to go further. I hope that with the new educational law this will change.

(Interview realized by Xabier Garagorri and Julie Bruneau)

4.4. Conceptual Perception 4: Interview with Prof. Jean-Jacques Chanaron, University of Grenoble France.

Professor Chanaron belongs to the group of foreign experts who supported the project Megatrend in all respects.

Professor Jean-Jacques Chanaron

The author: *How did you get familiar with Mića Jovanović?*

Prof. Chanaron: I met Mića at Berlin conference in 1987. My paper was CHANARON, J.J., (1987), Productivity and integration : methodological reflexions and empirical evidences, International Conference on The Future of Work in the Automobile Industry, WZB, Berlin, West Germany, 5-6 November 1987.

The author: *Why have you been so much involved in Megatrend University?*

Prof. Chanaron: We became friends as soon as we met on a personal basis and we were sharing the same values about teaching management in emerging countries. And of course, there is a historical proximity between Serbia and France.

The author: *How does the cooperation between your school and Megatrend work?*

Prof. Chanaron: We do have a MOU signed 10 years ago. The cooperation between the two schools of management has been difficult to develop since the economic situation in Serbia since the early 1990s does not allow local Serbian people to pay for their education in a Western university.

The author: *Please tell me some details about your commitment during the time of NATO bombing.*

Prof. Chanaron: During the war in the Balkans, I was teaching in Zastava automobile factory during the very first day of the war between Croatia and Serbia. Then, during the NATO bombing I was invited to teach not during the days of bombing but just before and just after the blitz on Belgrade.

The author: *What is your impression about development of Megatrend University you have served as President?*

Prof. Chanaron: I have been impressed by the growth in the volume of students, by the diversification towards new disciplines but I have been disappointed by the quality of the students when they get their degree. And I have been very disappointed by the failure of developing high value international degrees such as MBAs with top universities. My main critics would be on the very poor quality of the international partners and the refusal by international accreditations (AACSB, AMBA and EQUIS).

The author: *Did you help Megatrend to be included in TEMPUS Programme?*

Prof. Chanaron: Yes, I did indeed. The first MBA opened in Serbia (at that time Yugoslavia) was sponsored by Tempus for an executive MBA at Bor Mining Company and co-organized by my school (ESC Grenoble at that time) and Megatrend.

5. International Networking: EAMSA, NEWS, Direct Partnerships

The international inter-university cooperation usually consists of student and faculty exchange, holding of joint seminars, mutual recognition of academic degree, joint research projects, etc. Megatrend University has actively pursued this kind of cooperation. What is unique in Megatrend's inter-university cooperation is as follows: firstly, the establishment of Megatrend branch universities abroad such as London, Paris, etc.; secondly, the cooperation with Grenoble Business School (France), CERAM Sophia Antipolis (France), Changshin University (Korea), Berlin University of Applied Science, LUM Mediterranean University Bari, Italy, University II, Naples, Italy, Franklin University, USA, Technological Institute Monterey, Mexico, University of Economics, Slovakia, University Primorska Koper, Slovenia, etc. enables students of Megatrend University to continue study 1-2 years in exchange study program for an academic degree; lastly Megatrend University's membership in international academic associations which made student, especially professor exchange possible. In the following, two academic organizations which had been crucial for making Megatrend University known and ambassadors' lecture program which is new in Serbia will be described.

5.1. EAMSA (Euro-Asia Management Studies Association)

5.1.1. *A New Era for Intercultural Management:*

This academic organization was established for the purpose of focusing on intercultural management. The foundation of this organization goes back to the beginning of 1980s. Immensely increasing cross-border foreign direct investments by non-western MNCs from the beginning of 1980s necessitated the 'intercultural management' to deal more intensively with their widening scope and dimension. The demand for rather comprehensive expertise about intercultural management strategies and methods noticeably increased.

The surge in FDI especially by Japanese, Korean, Chinese and other Asian MNCs in Europe and the USA entailed necessity of elaborating new theoretical and methodological approach. Out of debates on more intensive cultural contacts between Europe/the West and Asia caused by FDI, the demand for dialogue of concerned scholars motivated approximately 30 scholars from Europe, Asia, and the USA to come together. In autumn of 1984, a workshop hosted by the Science Centre Berlin (Prof. Juergens) and the East-Asian Institute of Free University of Berlin (the author) was held. Scholars and experts came from Rotterdam, London, Tokyo, China, Serbia and Korea. The focus of this meeting was on initial research results on spread of Japanese foreign investments and management practices, and impediments and advantages that occurred during its transfer to European cultural context. One spoke then about the *challenge of Japanese management* which the Western management could hardly meet. Many European companies introduced some principles and techniques of Japanese management. Terminologies related to Japanese management such as Lean Production (Toyota production system), Kanban system (Just-in-Time), Kaizen, Suggestion system, QC circles, etc, were looming large. Universities set up Japanese management courses concurrently. Additionally, the companies originating from Japan expedited efforts to increase productivity by means of implementing Japanese management techniques in Europe. As a matter of fact, the Japanese management has been associated with pragmatic ingenuity for enhancing productivity of workforce.

In order to keep on discussions on spread of Japanese management in Europe and to improve the communication structure and the spread of information and exchange of research results among concerned scholars, the Euro-Japanese Management Studies Association (EJMSA) was founded." (see the website of EAMSA) The first president of EAMSA was a British scholar (Malcolm Trevor) of cultural anthropology researching then at a private institute in London. He wrote books and articles on the spread of Japanese management introduced by Japanese MNC's direct investment in UK. One of his books was "Under Japanese Management: Experience of British Workers (1983)". Facing massive FDI by Japanese MNCs in UK, this book was useful for those who dealt with Japanese management in practice as the first empirical *anthropological* field study suitable to 'look behind the truth of Japanese management'.

On the European continent, there were three groups dealing with the Japanese management: a Dutch group around Prof. Stam, Erasmus University of Rotterdam and another very strong group around Prof. Juergens and the author in Berlin. A huge project on "Industrial Relations in Japanese-invested companies in Germany" was financially supported by the Volkswagen Foundation. This group headed by the author made the first enquete on "Industrial Relations in Japanese-invested companies in Germany", of which the result was published under the title "Hans-Peter Merz/Sung-Jo Park: Japanisches Management in der Bundesrepublik Deutschland" (Express Edition: Berlin 1986). This book triggered many empirical studies on Japanese management in Germany and was regarded as a standard book. The second enquete was carried out 5 years later, by which in the meantime a shift from UK to West Germany took place. In West Germany, there were many conflicts between Japanese executives and German workforce in Japanese-invested companies caused by German laws of Co-Determination (cf. Sung-Jo Park, ed., Japanisches Management in der Bundesrepublik, Campus/Frankfurt 1991)

A propos the president of EJMSA, the author or Prof. Ulrich Juergens was expected by conference participants to assume presidency of the new Association as initiators of the Association. Both Berliners were hesitant to become the first president and proposed a British expert as the first president of the Association. Later it came out that he probably forgot to step down from the presidency by enjoying being at the top of the organization for 8 years. 8 years later, the author, one of the EAMSA initiators, succeeded to be the second president and the term of presidency became limited to two years.

5.1.2. The Rise of Asia Pacific and EAMSA:

The first conference of EAMSA in Asia was organized by the University of Tokyo in autumn of 1987 (Profs. Shibagaki and Abo). The contributions and discussions were concentrated on the topic of "Japanese and European Management: Their International Adaptability". At this meeting, in which about 100 researchers participated, the name of the Association was changed into the Euro-Asia Management Studies Association (EAMSA). This change was based on the proposal of Japanese scholars; interestingly neither Chinese nor Korean scholars initiated this proposal. The motivation of Japanese scholars to change the EJMSA's name might have been the fact that they took the massively increasing FDI by Japanese MNC's in East and Southeast Asia for worthy of particular attention. This tendency was to be seen also before the fast economic development of the Asian region as a whole, in particular, the Opening Policy of China. Thus, it was expected from EAMSA to take economic development of Asian economies and increase of FDI in this region into more consideration, engaging more experts and scholars from this region at the same time.

Summarizing the study trends of EAMSA, scholars concentrated on Japanese management in the 1980s, whilst on the economic development in China and India including NICS and Emerging Markets has been forming the core of study objects from the 1990s. Nevertheless, one cannot help stressing that full-fletched empirical studies on FDI in China and India are still missing.

The EAMSA today has more than 200 members from 30 different countries around the world. Roughly half of the members are from Asian countries. Members include scholars from leading academic institutions as well as executives, business consultants, researchers and Ph.D. students.

The website of EAMSA describes its aims as follows:

- *Promote research and education in the fields of business and management in Asia and Europe, with special emphasis on international comparisons.*
- *Foster an understanding of the role of international organizations and public policies in all matters related to Euro-Asian business activities.*
- *Encourage the exchange of research results, practical experience, and ideas by organizing conferences, meetings and developing research networks among members and institutions.*
- *Disseminate research results through various channels.'*

5.1.3. EAMSA and Megatrend University:

Megatrend University and EAMSA have been closely associated with each other from the beginning on in fourfold sense: firstly, Mića Jovanović as representative from Southeast Europe joined the first meeting of EAMSA in Berlin and soon became a member, thereafter a member of the advisory board. He was the only member of EAMSA from Southeast Europe. His contributions on system transformation in former socialist economies were highly appreciated; secondly, many of invited foreign lecturers later at Megatrend University were from EAMSA which practically meant that updated management knowledge and experiences of these lecturers could automatically flow into teaching at Megatrend University; thirdly, later the (second) chairman of EAMSA, the author became the first president of Megatrend University. He served as president for two years which obliged him to visit Belgrade frequently in order to join admission and commencement ceremonies. This fact that a foreign scholar assumed presidency at Megatrend University as a new school was really unique in the Balkan area. It was a great honor and challenge for him. The author was asked by mass media to give interviews, by which he always alluded to an optimistic prognosis of the Serbian manpower in the future. Further, he pointed to the fact that in former time before the Second World War, Serbia was a leading and the most developed republic within former Yugoslavia, which means that development and creativity potentials must have been accumulated and conserved in human resources. Now, the time arrived to find and develop them. Lastly, Mića Jovanović presented a paper at the 18th conference of EAMSA (2001) on "Megatrend University for System Transformation". All attendants were very much impressed by the success of Megatrend University in contributing to system transformation in Serbia.

Concluding the above-mentioned facts, it is quite understandable that Megatrend University's curriculum was updated meeting the West European standard, if not more advanced. Many scholars and experts the author met in Serbia were well-informed of this fact. The representative of Samsung Co. in Belgrade said to the author: "My son, student of Megatrend is learning the most advanced management theories and strategies in Serbia".

Despite the intensive ties between EAMSA and Megatrend University, it was not possible to organize an annual conference. Till now, most of the West European countries such as France, UK, Germany, Sweden, Netherlands, Italy, etc. hosted it. Without the Bosnian Crisis, an annual meeting could have been held in Serbia many years ago. EAMSA has had some traditions:

1) The conference has been held every year alternately in Europe and Asia.
2) Different from other associations, EAMSA has been publishing proceedings every year at renowned publishing companies, such as Palgrave McMillan, Routledge, University of Tokyo, Campus Frankfurt/New York etc.

In the following, EAMSA's publications are listed in order to show what kind of knowledge and information from EAMSA was produced and might have been intruded into contents of teaching at Megatrend University, in addition to the fact that some of these publications have been used as text books at Megatrend University.

Seoul Conference 2006

- Martin Hemmert (guest ed.): Emerging Economies in Asia: Inward and Outward Business Strategies. Special issue of Asian Business & Management, Vol. 7 (2008), No. 1.

Frankfurt (Oder) Conference 2005

- Wolfgang Dorow (ed.), The Transfer of Organisational Practices: Enhancing Competitiveness in Asia/Pacific - European Business Relationships? Proceedings of the 22nd Annual Conference of the Euro-Asia Management Studies Association, European University Viadrina, Frankfurt (Oder), Germany.

Hong Kong Conference 2004

- Yau, O.H.M. and Chow, R.P.M. (eds.), Harmony versus Conflict in Asian Business: Managing in a Turbulent Era, London: Palgrave Mcmillan, 2007. (ISBN 9780230542921)
- Oliver H.M. Yau, C.S. Tseng, Fany S.L. Cheung (eds.) Harmony v Conflict: Euro-Asian Management in a Turbulent Era? Proceedings of the 21th Annual Conference of the Euro-Asia Management Studies Association, City University of Hong Kong, Hong Kong SAR (ISBN 962-442-259-1, Conference Proceedings, 2004).

Stockholm Conference 2003

- Sten Sherman (ed.), Emerging Multiplicity: Integration and Responsiveness in Asian Business Development, London: Palgrave McMillan, 2006. (ISBN 1-4039-9176-6)
- Sten Sherman (ed.), Local Responsiveness versus Global Integration? Proceedings of the 20th Annual Conference of the Euro-Asia Management Studies Association. Stockholm University, Stockholm, Sweden (ISBN 91-631-4539-1, Conference Proceedings, 2003).

Bangkok Conference 2002

- Axel Giroud, Alex T. Mohr, Deli Yang (eds.), Multinationals and Asia: Organizational and Institutional Relationships, London and New York: Routledge/Curzon, 2005. (ISBN 0-415-343232)
- Hafiz Mirza, Axel Giroud, Deli Yang and Alexander Mohr (eds.), competition and Cooperation in Asia and Europe : Corporate and Government Perspectives and Strategies? Proceedings of the 19th Annual Conference of the Euro-Asia Management Studies Association. Chulalongkorn University, Bangkok, Thailand (ISBN 1-85143-191-8, Conference Proceedings, 2002).

Berlin Conference 2001

- Sung-Jo Park, Sierk Horn (eds.), Asia and Europe in the New Global System: Intercultural Cooperation and Competition Scenarios, London and New York: Palgrave, 2003

Singapore Conference 2000

- Hellmut Schuette (ed.): The Localisation and the Uniqueness of Asia? Proceedings of the 17th Annual Conference of the Euro-Asia Management Studies Association. INSEAD, Asia Campus, Singapore 2000.

Rotterdam Conference 1999

- Joop A. Stam (Guest Editor): Economy and Business in Asia: Post-Crisis Perspectives, Management International Review, vol. 42, special issue 1, 2002.

Taipei Conference 1998

- Po-Young Chu (eds.): Industrial Economics and Knowledge Center/ Industrial Technology Research Institute R.O.C. (eds.): Industry Forum Journal, EAMSA Special Issue, January 2002.
- Po-Young Chu, Da-Nien Liu and Ching-Sung Wu (eds.), Collaboration Between Europe and Asia ? Proceedings of the 15th Annual Conference of the Euro-Asia Management Studies Association. Taipei-Hsinchu, Republic of China. 1998.

Metz Conference 1997

- Jacques Liouville (ed.), Asian Firms Looking Towards the Global Market? Proceedings of the 14th Annual Conference of the Euro-Asia Management Studies Association. Metz, France. (Conference Proceedings, 1997).

Tokyo Conference 1996

- Yoshiaki Takahashi, Minoru Murata, Khondaker M. Rahman (eds.): Management Strategies of Multinational Corporations in Asian Markets. Tokyo: Chuo University Press, 1998.

Milano Conference 1995

- Lucrezia Songini (ed.): Political and Economic Relations between Asia and Europe. Milano: EGEA 2000.

Kedah Conference 1994

- Mohamad Hanapi Mohamad (coord. ed.): Malaysian Management Journal, Vol. 2, No. 1 + 2, 1997.

Nuernberg Conference 1993

- Briji N. Kumar (guest ed.): Euro-Asian Management and Business I + II. Management International Review, Special Issue 1/95 and 2/95.
- Brij N. Kumar and Harald Dolles (eds.), New Management Concepts and Changing Managerial Roles in Euro-Asia Business, Diskussionsbeitrag des Lehrstuhls fuer Betriebswirtschaftslehre insbesondere Internationales Management (Prof. Dr. Brij N. Kumar), Friedrich-Alexander-Universitaet Erlangen-Nuernberg, no. 3., 1993. (ISSN 0945-0610-x)

Bradford Conference 1992

- Hafiz Mirza (ed.): Global Competitive Strategies in the World Economy. Cheltenham: Edward Elgar, 1998.

Fontainebleau Conference 1991

- Helmut Schuette (ed.): Global Competitiveness of the Asian Firm, Houndsmill: MacMillan, 1994.

Berlin Conference 1990

- Sung Jo Park (ed.): Managerial Efficiency in Competition and Cooperation, Frankfurt: Campus-Westview, 1992.

Nagoya Conference 1989

- Malcolm H. Trevor (ed.): International Business and the Management of Change. Euro-Asian Perspectives. Aldershot: Avebury-Gover, 1991.

Beer Sheva Conference 1988

- Tuvia Blumenthal (ed.): Employer and Employee in Japan and Europe . Beer Sheva: Ben Gurion University/Negev Press, 1989.

Tokyo Conference 1987

- Kazuo Shibagaki/Tetsuo Abo/Malcolm H. Trevor (eds.): Japanese and European Management: Their International Adaptability, Tokyo: University of Tokyo Press, 1989.

Rotterdam Conference 1986

- Joop A. Stam (ed.): Industrial Cooperation between Europe and Japan, Rotterdam: Erasmus University Press, 1990.

London Conference 1985

- Malcolm H. Trevor (ed.): Internationalization of Japanese Business, Frankfurt: Campus/Westview, 1987.

Berlin Conference 1984

- Sung Jo Park/Ulrich Juergens/Hans-Peter Merz (eds.): Transfer des japanischen Managementsystems, Berlin: Express Edition, 1985.

The thematic spectrum of EAMSA annual conference has greatly changed in the meantime. In the beginning years, one placed more focus on economic aspects of foreign direct investments and transfer of management principles and techniques by MNCs from advanced countries. In the recent time, studies are concentrating on a variety of themes encompassing cultural, social, and environmental variables, mostly in statistical and quantitative methodology in close cooperation with the journal "Asia Business & Management" (Palgrave).

5.2. Global University Network (NEWS)

5.2.1. From Bilateralism to Multilateralism

In 1970s and 1980s, the university international cooperation was understood as comprising exchange of students and teaching staff. In the meantime, demand for widening and deepening inter-university cooperation increased. This trend was accelerated by globalization in the beginning 1990s. Above all, after the end of the Cold War and the fall of Berlin Wall in 1989, people were motivated to integrate socialist education system into the western capitalistic market-centered education system. This tendency was looming large especially in East Germany which had advantages compared to other socialist economies: West German universities were involved in helping East German universities, first by replacing so-called 'communist-regime-friendly' professors by West German professors, and East German curriculum by West German university ones. However, those former socialist economies lacking even this possibility were in a great difficulty. The author, Prof. Jahnke from Berlin University of Applied Science and some other professors took initiative to create a forum of universities and professors from former socialist economies and from Western economies. Representatives of both economies came together in the 1990s in order to find concepts and ways for efficiently helping universities in former socialist economies by means of finding cooperation partner for student and faculty member exchange, for joint research work, holding joint seminars, etc.

To be precise, the scope of cooperation consisted of

a. exchange of students;
b. exchange and joint supervision of doctoral students;
c. exchange of researchers and faculty;
d. exchange of scientific, academic, and technical information and appropriate academic materials and other information of mutual interest.

In the past, the inter-university cooperation between western universities was carried out *bilaterally*. The paradigm change behind widening of bilateral inter-university cooperation was to create *multilateral* cooperation. This could be realized easily when representatives of cooperation-seeking universities came together on a *multi-university cooperation forum* and reached a cooperation agreement. Herein the Global University Network was seen as the main task primarily following the goal to enable universities to promote *multilateral cooperation.* After the fall of Berlin wall, former socialist economies embarked on change from socialist to capitalist economy first from the institutional, legal and organizational standpoint of view. Then, universities in former socialist countries were assigned to bring up market-economy-adequate human resources. However, they were faced with difficulties to find pertinent cooperation partner in the West. Taking Megatrend University as a brand-new university from a former socialist country, the Global University Network provided a useful forum for finding proper cooperation partners.

Universities from China, Russia, East Germany, etc. which joined the Global University Network benefited a lot from cooperation with i.e. Changshin University (South Korea) and Berlin University of Applied Sciences, Zuerich University of Applied Sciences, etc.

In the meantime, the composition of members and goals of Global University Network changed. The member universities from socialist and capitalist economies are in a well-balanced proportion. Finding a cooperation partner is a task not only for universities from former socialist economies, but also universities from capitalist economies. They are taking efforts to pursue human resources development projects jointly with partners from former socialist economies in order to meet demand on globalizing market. The projects in this cooperation framework would be regarded as *'development projects'* which are supported by UN-related agencies and development aid agencies of advanced countries. This tendency has gained great importance in inter-university cooperation in the recent time.

To exemplify one project in this context, the University of Mongolia in Ulan Bataar is intending to get a cyber university with software, technology and a full set of equipment financed by KOICA (Korean International Cooperation Agency).The project is to amount to more than some million US dollars for several years. For pursuing this project, the Mongolian University needs a partner university to accompany the project concerned. Representatives of the Mongolian University (Prof. Batsuk Davaasuren, Head of International Trade and Marketing Dept.) and Sejong University (President Park Woo-Hee) on the Korea side came together at last 8th Global University Network Meeting in Yichang (China). Negotiations were begun. It seems at the moment that the project concerned can be eventually materialized in the near future.

At the current stage, the Global University Network, whose 8th annual meeting was held in 2011 at China Three Gorges University, is researching the following possibilities in order to deepen inter-university cooperation. Striking was the fact that especially those universities located in 'remote areas' such as Iceland, Africa, Oceania, and South America have shown interest in Global University Network. Also, other specific-subject-centered discussion forum emerged. For instance, scholars of marketing from East Asia came together in order to set up "East Asia Marketing Association". A representative of a Chinese University proposed "Asia Pacific Academic Elite Forum" modeled after the Davos Forum which is scheduled to be held in Yanji, China in 2012.

The following items were intensively discussed at the 8th Conference.

- identification of opportunities for cooperation and joint research and development in disciplines of mutual interest;
- identification of and support for joint research proposals
- identification of opportunities for the commercialization of technology; and
- the organization and participation in joint academic and scientific activities such as seminars and conferences.

The Global University Network has been called NEWS. This abbreviation is standing for **n**orth, **e**ast, **w**est and **s**outh which is meant to be tantamount to four global directions. The author proposed this abbreviation. Since the terminology 'global' was not so popular at the beginning of 1990s, the member universities of Global University Network preferred to use NEWS. NEWS has become a symbol for universities interested in *multilateral inter-university cooperation.*

5.2.2. *NEWS as a Political or Non-political Club?*

In the following, a brief history about NEWS as a political or non-political club will be described. At the Masan Meeting in Korea in 1994 there was a disagreeably boring discussion. Some German representatives doubted about Megatrend University's membership eligibility, because at that time, the Bosnian Crisis was in full swing and many West Europeans thought that Slobodan Milosevic was responsible for the Bosnian Crisis and that all Serbian people were supporting this dictator. The person who strongly opposed to Megatrend's membership of NEWS was President of Berlin University of Applied Science. Prof. Dusan Jokanovic (Megatrend University) tried to find some arguments in favor of his university's membership eligibility of NEWS, but in vain. He was isolated. The atmosphere of that meeting was heated and nobody tried to defend the position of Prof. Jokanovic. Obviously, his argument was very carefully formulated in order not to be exposed to suspicion of being contra the Milosevic regime. The author interfered and tried to argue that the NEWS meeting is a *non-political* one and thus should place a great accent on defending and integrating our colleagues working under current extremely difficult political condition. Seeing that NEWS should follow non-political goals, the agreement was reached to include our colleagues of Serbia as well and not to isolate them.

This argument seemed to persuade President of Berlin University of Applied Science and other West European colleagues. Nevertheless, Prof. A. said to the author. "He should still abide by his political judgment on Serbia". For him it was the first time to notice that there were reservations among German colleagues concerning inclusion of universities of certain countries which were known to be 'aggressive in their foreign relations'. However, by using the 'aggressiveness in foreign relations' as membership eligibility criteria, for instance, all universities of China would have been very problematic for membership.

5.2.2.1. A Christian University in China

The Third meeting was held in China by YUST (Yanbian University of Science and Technology) in 1996. This is a university which was built up as a Chinese-American joint venture in Yanji, China. The founder is an American of Korean origin, Prof. James Kim. It is very interesting that the financing of this university came from Christian churches of Korea, also partly from other churches of overseas Koreans in the USA, Canada, etc. Christian organizations from Germany and France made donations to this university. Especially, German Christian missionary organizations were strongly supportive of this University in terms of cash and sending teachers and professors, some of whom are still working at this university.

The goal of this university was primarily to bring up young people in the spirit of Christianity. To be more precise, this university aimed at missionary activity has not been pursued publicly in China. Since the missionary activity has been prohibited in China, the university has been striving to educate young Chinese in Christian creed. Some professors are proud that many Chinese students have been converted to Christianity. Superficially, it looked as if all teaching staff at this University worked on voluntary basis. In reality, professors and other teaching staffs were financially supported by their own mentor churches or Christian organizations. It means that this university has been closely interwoven with missionary activities of Christian organizations and churches in South Korea, the USA, Canada, Japan etc. At any rate, the university had to pay attention to strict surveillance by the Chinese Communist Party. Once and again the party secretary residing at the university campus frankly said to the author that "this university would be thorny for the eyes of Chinese Communist Party." However, in the meantime, a surprising change on Chinese side took place. In the past, the Sunday church service was carried out in a secret space. Some years ago, the Chinese side allowed sunday church service in the main auditorium of the university. Now, the university set up a church building at the university campus. It is not certain whether this lenient policy by the Chinese Communist Party towards the Christian religion at this campus can be interpreted as a gradual liberalization of 'freedom of religion' at least in the city of Yanji.

Many people ask how this university came to its foundation in Yanji, far away from the central region of China. There is a very interesting story. Prof. James Kim, founder of YUST asked the author at the beginning of 1980s whether he knew powerful persons in China. He recommended Prof. Lo Chengchi, former president of the Chinese Academy of Social Sciences and the Institute of World Economy to him. The author made acquaintance with him during his Harvard Visiting Professorship in Boston in 1982-1983. After his return to Berlin, he invited Prof. Lo to give a special lecture at the international conference (1985) financed by the Berlin Government "21st century – the Asian Century?". He was one of the five invited speakers such as Ishida Takeshi (Tokyo University), Johan Galtung (Princeton University), Park Woo-Hee (Seoul National University) and Arthur Stockwin (Oxford University). His speech was on "World Economic Trends and their Impact on

Developing Countries with Special Reference to China". After this speech, he gave some lectures at Free University of Berlin spending almost one month for lecture tours in West Germany. Since then, Prof. Lo and the author came closer to each other, having edited and published books and journals. Above all, Prof. Lo, and the author with some others took an initiative to begin with publication of a journal "EAST ASIA" (International Review of Economic, Political and Social Development) (Publisher Campus Frankfurt/ New York) in 1983. This was the first periodical dealing with the economic and political rise of the Asia-Pacific on the European continent.

On the recommendation of the author, Prof. James Kim met Prof. Lo in Beijing who helped Prof. Kim a lot in building up a university in Yanji. At that time, it was really unthinkable for foreigners to set up a private university in China, even though this project was declared as an American-Chinese Joint Venture. Prof. Lo's *guanxi (*in Chinese term: relationship, network*)* must have made great contribution to alleviating many kind of difficulties in opening a private university. Prof. Kim was offered a huge land (for 99 years' lease contract with the city administration of Yanji) at the top of a hill having a wonderful overview on the Yanji city.

The city Yanji with a half million population is a sort of Mecca of Korean minority located in the triangle between China, North Korea and Russia. Prof. Kim nominated the author for vice president for international affairs. His function was to organize international conferences, fund raising, student and faculty exchange. He could create contact between this university and German Christian institutions like EKD (Evangelische Kirche Deutschland), Brot fuer die Welt, Caritas, etc., so that some financial assistance was granted by these organizations to the university. Further, student exchange could be realized with partner universities in Germany, Korea and Switzerland. Especially, students of Yanji studied first at Berlin University of Applied Sciences, and then at Berlin Institute of Technology where some of these students succeeded in receiving Ph.D. degree.

Hearing about Yanji in China everyone would ask where it is located. Who could imagine that someone establishes a university in that remote area from the central region of China, a triangle between Russia, China and North Korea? On top of it, a private university! The founder Prof. Kim is in certain sense comparable to Prof. Mića Jovanović. Both of them have chosen an unusual way in establishing a university. The author was heavily involved in internationalization of his university in terms of holding international conferences. He organized international conferences 7 times. His efforts were to bring renowned universities and colleges to Yanji such as Berlin University of Applied Sciences, Zuerich University of Applied Sciences, Seoul National University, Nihon University, China Peoples University, Megatrend University, China Three Gorges University, Changshin University Korea etc. All these universities entered into cooperation with Yanbian University of Science and Technology and actively pursued student exchange. Some students from Yanji went to Berlin, Zuerich and Korea for further study.

Every Spring, the *international* conference was seen as a feast for professors and students for three days. Many foreigners visited this university and this area. Some of them got informed of the famous UNDP-Tumen Project and could visit the Economic Special Zone in North Korea Rajin-Sunbong (Rasun). For conference participants, a tour to Rajin-Sunbong (now Rasun) in North Korea was organized. Even though this city was declared as 'Economic Free Zone', noticeable investments were not carried out by foreign firms. We could witness how poor North Koreans were.

The major part of inhabitants in this area is the Korean minority. The history of this minority is going back to the Japanese colonialism which pursued a forced migration of Korean workforce to this region for land development and coal mining. After the Second World War, this minority got settled down as the main economic factor and the Chinese government conferred administrative autonomy on this minority. They were oriented preferably towards North Korea in the past due to geographical proximity to North Korea till about 20 years ago. Since South Korea with its increasing economic prosperity has been trying to open towards communist countries from the end of 1980s, an economically very close relation between this region and South Korea including the daily direct flight connection between Seoul and Yanji has developed. More than 0.2 Million people from this region are actually Gastarbeiter in South Korea.

Since the author stepped down from the vice presidency of YUST in Yanji, the international conference was changed to a "Korean-Chinese Conference" which means that the absolutely major part of conference attendants comes from Korea. This is because Koreans have chance to visit this place in order to climb up to the Baiktu Mountain (*changbai shan*) which has a mythological symbol for the foundation of Korea 4 thousand years ago.

5.2.3. *NEWS and Megatrend University in the Future*

Megatrend University was expected to delegate 4 professors to the 8th Annual Meeting hosted by China Three Gorges University (CTGU) in September 19-22, 2011. More than 25 universities such as the Private Engineering School of Lille, France, Vienna University of Applied Science, University of Vienna, Nihon University, University of Texas (Dallas), Siam University, Amur State University, Hubei Institute of Technology, National University of Mongolia, etc. witnessed the rapid internationalization of CTGU, into which the former Agricultural University, the Educational College and the Technical College in Yichang merged. Due to its adjacency to the biggest dam in the world, "Three Gorges Dam", which in addition to production of an immense volume of electricity, serves to keep the Yangtse River from flood, this university is said to be one of the most favorite infrastructure projects by the Chinese government. CTGU was greatly privileged to receive generous financial support from the Central and Provincial Government, especially for the reason that many families were evacuated from the Yangtse River area due to the dam construction and forcibly resettled in river areas. Children of those families were granted opportunity to study here at CTGU.

The first day of the conference was devoted to the question of how the Global University Network can be more intensified. For this purpose, a new chairman and new General Secretary were elected. The second day was contributed to International Workshop on "Higher Education in Knowledge Economy", where excellent papers on reform of higher education in different countries were presented.

The next conference was planned to be held in Seoul, May 27-30, 2012. The hosting university is the renowned private University Sejong.

With the development of Global University Network, one can notice following trends:

1. Increasing activities of universities and higher education institutions: In the past, the inter-university cooperation was mostly likely to be left to universities in advanced countries. In recent times, universities from less developed countries join inter-university cooperation meeting asking for concrete cooperation projects.

2. Nowadays, the bilateral inter-university cooperation concentrating on student and faculty exchange and recognition of credit points is replaced by joint academic degree, joint research and joint summer or winter school, further establishing branch university etc.
3. An interesting trend of NEWS is Summer or/and Winter University. Especially, Chinese universities have been eargerly striving to host Summer University, whereas Korean Universities a Winter University. Students used to go to Summer or Winter University to advanced countries in the USA and Europe. However, this tendency is changing. Instead, Chinese universities are gaining more importance. CTGU's Summer University is recommendable to foreign students.

5.3. Direct partnerships, Ambassador Lectures and Other International Events Participation

Direct Partnerships

Megatrend University has direct partnership relationships with a number of foreign universities and institutions (see also Appendix 1)

- A joint international doctorate program was launched in 2008 among Libera Universita Mediterranea Jean Monnet, Italy, Megatrend University, Serbia and University Alma Mater, Romania. The topic of this doctorate program is "Economics and Management of Natural Resources".
- Joint work in scientific programs that include the exchange of professors, students and publications has been established with University of Primorska, from Koper, Slovenia. So far, 4 student workshops have been organized on the topic of the Balkan Interculturalism.
- Within the cooperation agreement signed with Instituto Tecnologico y de Estudios Superiores de Monterrey, the Institute provides 2 scholarships per year for Megatrend University students. Those scholarships are based on the six-months-research-

scientific work, organized as a joint project between the students of Megatrend University and the Institute of Monterrey and is carried out within its campus in Mexico.

- In March 2010, the agreement was signed between Graduate School of Business Studies, Megatrend University and the Technological Educational Institute of Serres, Greece. The cooperation is based on student mobility and internships, as well as joint educational, research and European programs.
- The cooperation agreement was signed between Megatrend University and Universidad de Alcala de Henares, Spain, according to which, Megatrend students would spend a part of their studies in Belgrade and another part in Spain. Upon successful completion of the program, students obtain a diploma from both institutions.
- Other institutions that the Megatrend University has cooperation with include: West University of Timisoara, Romania, University of Pecs, Hungary, Ortega y Gasset Research Institute, Madrid, Spain, St. Ivan Rilski, Bulgaria, Mediterranean University of Podgorica, Montenegro, L'Ecole Superieure de Commerce, Grenoble, France, Universidad de Chile, Santiago de Chile, Universidad El Salvador, Argentina, Yanbian University of Science and Technology, China, Russian Academy of Science, Moscow, Russia, Universidad Simon Bolivar, Caracas, Venezuela, and St Petersburg State University of State and Economy, Russia.

Lectures by Foreign Ambassadors

Universities located in capital cities have a great advantage to accede to foreign embassies and other foreign MNCs. American and German universities have the tradition to invite foreign ambassadors to give lectures.

Megatrend University as the first university in Serbia continually invites the ambassadors of foreign countries in Serbia and they deliver lectures related to contemporary economic, political and social trends in their home countries. Although these lectures are primarily aimed at Megatrend University students, they are also open for the wider public and offer the opportunity of broadening knowledge, as well as interaction and developing relationships in international scene.

Recently, Megatrend University has had the honor to welcome the ambassadors of Argentina, Venezuela, Brazil, Peru, Japan, Russia, Sweden, Austria, France, U.S.A., Canada, etc.

Organization and Participation in International Events:

Megatrend University is very active in organizing and participating in international events. One of the very successful events organized by the Megatrend University is the International Canadian Conference organized every second year and supported by the Ministry of Education, Republic of Serbia. In addition to that, the International Scientific Conference (10 years of tradition) that takes place every year in November at Megatrend University is very influential.

6. Megatrend Virtual University (MTVU)

(special contribution by Prof. Veljko Spasic)

Prof. Dr Veljko Spasić, research counselor
Director of Megatrend Virtual University
UNESCO-UN consultant

Megatrend Virtual University – MTVU
http://www.megatrend-online.com

Origin and Development of the Idea

During the eighties of the last century, Mića Jovanović was in London, at the London School of Economics where he was working on his Ph.D. thesis.

At the same time, Veljko Spasić was also in London where he was working at the London University – King's College as an invited researcher in the central team of the British National Project CAL (Computer Assisted Learning) performing research and development in CAL, primarily based on the methods of artificial intelligence and mathematical modeling and simulation

Besides doctoral dissertation, which he diligently worked on from 1980 to 1983 at the London School of Economics (in collaboration with Council for National Academic Awards), Prof. Dr Jovanović was developing the concept of real system management based on the knowledge management via distributive approach. This approach led him to the idea that it is necessary to develop diversified schooling system that would be nationally positioned in several cities, not only in one center, and that would support high university level of traditionally established and new knowledge, but at the same time be elastic and capable to follow dynamic scientific development. That is how the idea was born, the idea that would later, with a many-years effort, become Megatrend University (http://www.megatrend.edu.rs), today's biggest private university at the south-east of Europe, the university with many colleges located in many cities over the country at the "front doors" of the students.

Along the same period, during his research at the King's College, Prof. Dr Veljko Spasić was gradually developing the idea of possible widespread application of the computer potentials in the field that can be defined as "Computer and Learning". The idea was to base the complex process of learning on the computer by using dedicated, adaptive, specially developed software. The whole system would be delivered directly to students. This was the idea that, even in those early days, could have been named as "virtual university". Prof. Spasic, following that concept, wrote extensive software for that virtual university. But, the global delivering media was still not developed. It was necessary to wait.

Friendship and initial steps in collaboration between the two researchers originate from London. After returning to Belgrade and several years later, they continued to discuss about the possibility of implementing virtual university project. Now, the project was realistic because in the meanwhile, Internet was developed. It was clear that the fast development is ahead.

The concept had the name *InterTrans*(c) (Internet based knowledge transfer) and its pilot implementation in the form of virtual university got the name Megatrend Virtual University – MTVU (http://www.megatrend-online.com).

MTVU was promoted in the USA at the international e-learning congress where over 80 countries participated. Many compliments were given to the MTVU mainly for the original approach. It was the first Internet based virtual university in Yugoslavia and in this part of Europe[1].

MTVU Concept

Basic educational concept which is the core of *InterTrans*(c) system and its MTVU implementation could be characterized as *guided discovery.*

Within this concept, integrated as one system, various knowledge transfer modalities are simultaneously present. Each of them contributes to the more efficient learning. In the Table *InterTrans concept*, educational approaches are shown along with the corresponding implementation.

---

[1] ***Spasić, A.V. (1998),*** *SKOLEX - Artificial Intelligence Approach in CAL.* Proc. of The Fifteenth International Conf. on Technology and Education, Santa Fe, USA, Martch 1998, pp 103-107.
Spasić, A.V. (1998), *Virtual Experiment - The Essential Role of Simulation in CAL.* Proc. of The Fifteenth International Conf. on Technology and Education, Santa Fe, USA, March 1998, 178-182.
Spasić, A.V. (2000), *Self-Explaining Learning Environment*, Proc. of the 18 ICTE International Conf., Johanesburg, South Africa, April 2000.
Spasić, A.V. (2000), *Intelligent Virtual Systems in Learning*, Proc. World Congress of Biomedical Engineering, Chicago, USA, 2000, 462-466.
Spasić, A.V. (2001), *InterTrans – Concept and Implementation of the First Virtual University in Yugoslavia*, Proc. of the 19 ICTE International Conf., Tallahassee, Florida, USA, May 2001.
Spasić, A.V. (2001), *InterCons – Intelligent Internet Based Consultative System*, Proc. of the 19 ICTE International Conf., Tallahassee, Florida, USA, May 2001.
http://www.megatrend-online.com/cv_prof_dr_veljko_spasic.pdf

	InterTrans©	
EDUCATIONAL APPROACH	↔	**CORRESPONDING IMPLEMENTATION**
Lecture based learning	↔	Multimedia lessons- lectures
Consultative learning	↔	**InterCons©** Adaptive Virtual Professor-Consultant
Consultative learning	↔	Multipurpose synchronous and asynchronous connections with the real professor
xperiment based learning	↔	**InterLab©** Virtual laboratory
Discussion based learning	↔	On-Line discussion forum
Learning based on assignments	↔	Tests, exercises, seminar papers, references, Internet links
Additional support: MTVU info, bulletin boards, references, news, guest books, help,….		

Table: *InterTrans concept*

It is self-evident from the Table which learning modalities are incorporated. But, it should be stressed that implementation is the essence of the InterTrans(c) and MTVU.

MTVU will not be presented here completely. Among all the components of MTVU, only one, possibly the most original one, will be described in details – subsystem for consultative learning. This is a part of the concept which supports MTVU functioning very efficiently.

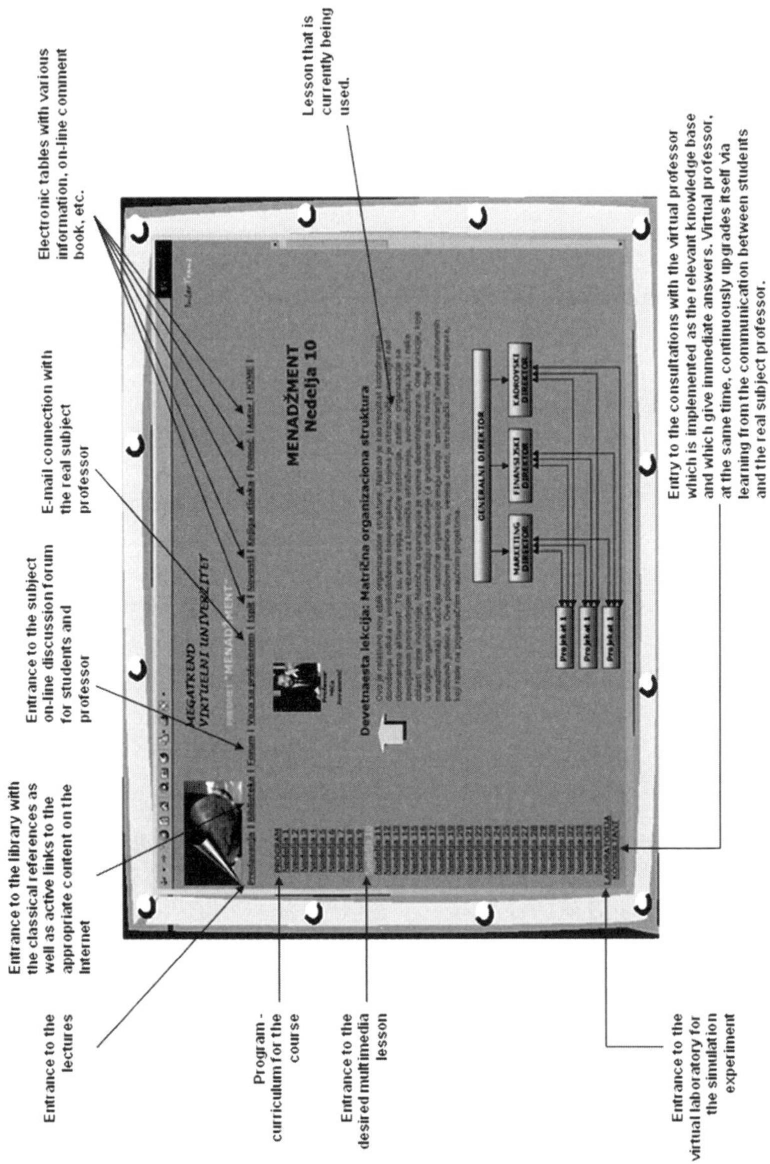

MTVU Home Page at the Internet with explanations

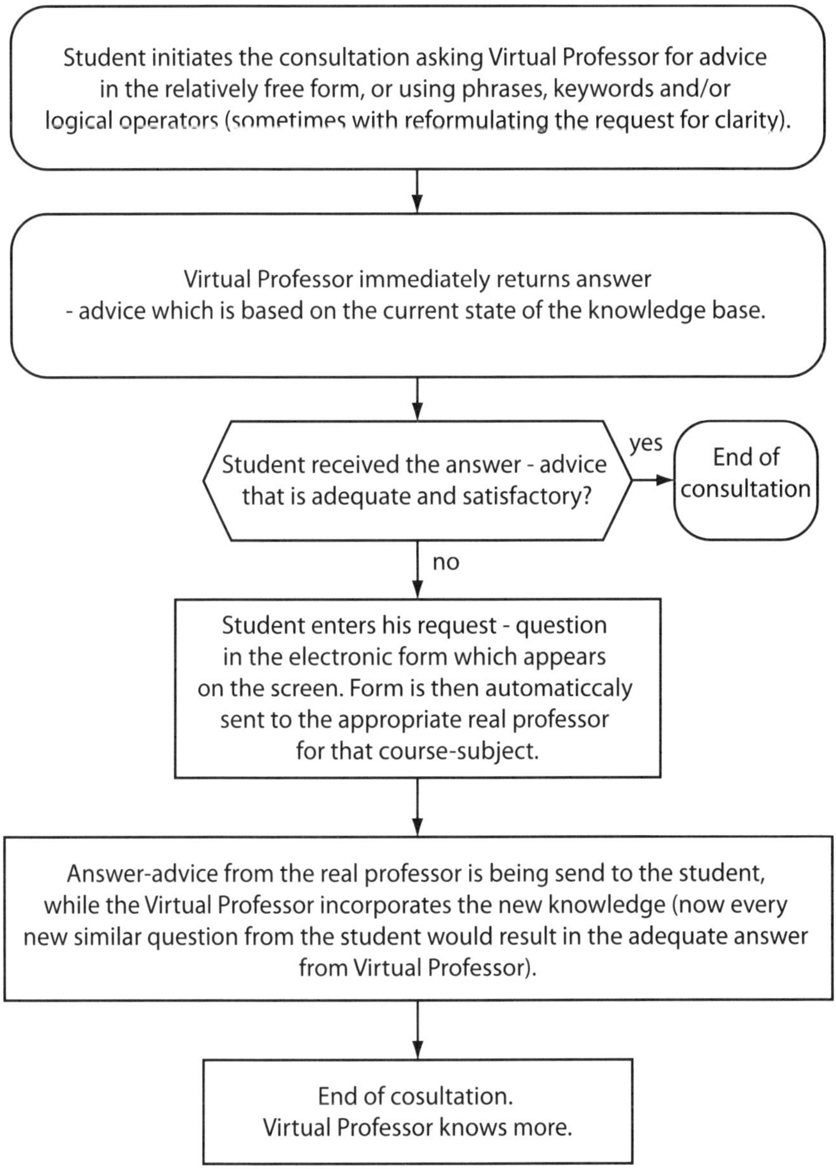

Consultation flow diagram

Virtual Consultative Professor

One of the basic problems in attempt to define the system for knowledge transfer via Internet is the balance between synchronous and a synchronous subsystems. Synchronous (on-line) approach is based on interactivity, direct on-line Internet access, as well as simultaneous Internet presence of student and professor. Asynchronous (off-line) approach is an obstacle for the student-professor interactivity, but in that case, they do not have to be simultaneously present on the Internet. Both approaches have advantages and disadvantages that are apparent, but will not be discussed here.

Synchronous - asynchronous dilemma, in the concept of *InterTrans*, led to the original introduction of intermediate approach which harmonizes mentioned advantages and disadvantages. The idea got a name *Virtual Professor-Consultant* and is implemented as a subsystem called *InterCons*(c). In short, it is the virtual simulation of consultative learning.

Virtual Professor-Consultant is constructed as a subsystem with its own knowledge from the appropriate subject-course, a subsystem that responds to students' requests. But at the same time, it is capable to adapt and acquire new knowledge during the consultation when no adequate answer could be obtained. Virtual Professor is coupled with the knowledge base. Each subject-course that is implemented in MTVU has unique Virtual Professor with appropriate knowledge (construction of this resource is very substantial and is academically a difficult task).

During the consultative process, student sends his consultative requests-questions in the relatively free form, or by using phrases, keywords and/or logical operators. Virtual Professor returns answer-advice. If the student is satisfied, he can finish the consultation. If not, student can send the same question to the real professor who supports the course. Student receives the answer, Virtual Professor incorporates the new knowledge, in other words, it learns in line with the students' requests.

Consultative process between student and Virtual Professor is presented in the form of block diagram on Fig. *Consultation flow diagram.* Some of the main Virtual Professor characteristics are:

- open field of applications;
- adaptive growth of knowledge;
- synchronous availability for anyone who is in Virtual amphitheatre;

- instant response;
- easy usage based on the clear interface;
- parallel (simultaneous) service to the large number of students.

In the Virtual amphitheatre, besides the links to lectures, there is always a link to Virtual Professor. In that way, virtual consultative learning is available to students at any moment.

It should be noted that one Virtual Professor, developed for one course, easily and instantly covers simultaneous consultations with many students. Also, over the time, the role of the real professor is being reduced, while the role of Virtual Professor, which continuously widens the knowledge, is gradually being increased.

Chronology of Development

Development of MTVU took several phases, from idea, over to implementation, then testing, running and after that periodical development and maintenance. Time necessary to finish each of the phases is measured in years due to the complexity and size of MTVU.

The most important steps along the implementation and function of MTVU could be roughly defined and positioned on time scale in the following order:

1999

- Development of the idea and conception
- Publication of the related papers

2000–2001

- Development of MTVU
- Programming
- Uploading onto servers
- Final testing
- Promotion in the USA

2002

- Running of MTVU version 2002/2003
- Maintenance
- Promotion in Belgrade

2003

- Development, testing and running of the new MTVU version 2003/04
- Maintenance

2004

- Development, testing and running of the new MTVU version 2004/05
- Maintenance

2005

- Development, testing and running of the new MTVU version 2005/06
- Maintenance

2006

- Development, testing and running of the new MTVU version 2006/07
- Maintenance

2007...

Period that was finished in 1999 had a span of many years and resulted in paper publications where parts of the MTVU concept were presented, as well as some original solutions for the MTVU problems.

On Fig. *Time scale of MTVU development,* MTVU chronology (of idea, publications, development, implementation, testing, maintenance..) is presented.

Professors Jovanović and Spasic (2007).

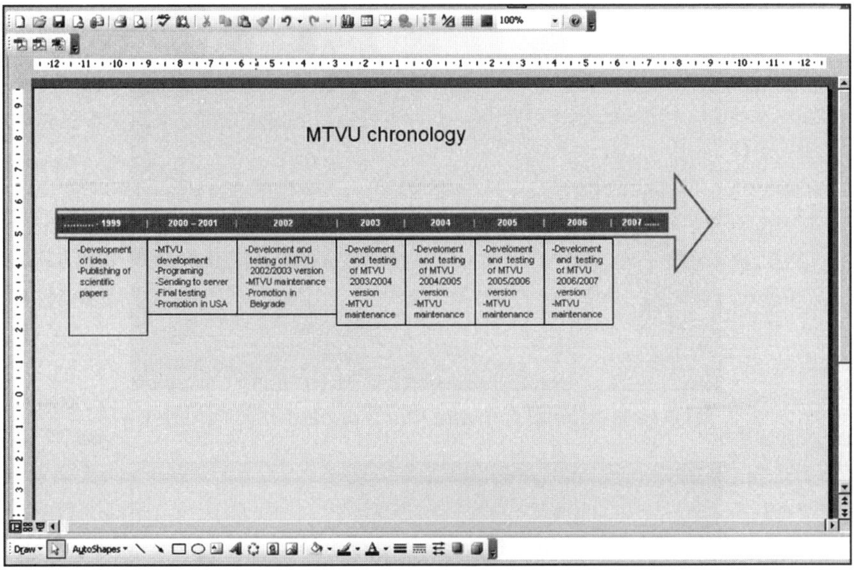

Time scale of MTVU development

Analysis of MTVU Results

MTVU currently has 174 virtual courses in continuous function. Printed MTVU software code has reached substantially more than 100 volumes, each over 500 printed pages.

MTVU has several successive versions of curriculum because it is necessary to allow students to finish the study with their initial program if there is a curriculum change or even deeper education system reform.

It is interesting that MTVU has been operating continuously without breaks or server down for many years now. This, for domestic standards, is certainly a surprising fact and is the result of several good solutions and decisions in information technology domain, but as well as the result of good MTVU daily maintenance organization development strategies.

Frequency of the students' connections is very high, even higher during the weekend days. Also, during the weekday, there is a large number of connected students in the evenings than the rest of the day, and interestingly, there is one peak around 3 am. Who can say that the young generation is lazy?

MTVU has original software that is printed in 96 volumes.

After the promotion of printed MTVU software –
Prof. Dr Mića Jovanović (right) and Prof. Dr Veljko Spasić (left)

In the anonymous student pool where students were asked to rank the general quality of MTVU using the academic scale from 5 to 10, the obtained average mark was 9.1.

There was a great satisfaction when the results of multi-year analysis of MTVU average student exam grade revealed that the MTVU students have the average exam grades higher than "classic" students. The difference between those two groups was 0.2 in favour of MTVU students.

Quality

The analysis of the MTVU quality is performed via several methods. One of them is the pooling the students. The questions are related to the quality of the MTVU's various parameters and approaches, and then the students' answers are grouped and analyzed.

Pooling is being continuously made using Internet based electronic forms incorporated within the MTVU.

In the Table on next page, the results of the recent pool are displayed. Grades are on the academic scale from 5 to 10.

Table presents average results as well as the average of all obtained average results. Results vary from 7.2 to 9.2. Two worst grades are obtained for the questions: *"Are discussion forums useful?"* (7,26) and *"Grade the balance between theoretical and practical approach in MTVU courses"* (7,42), while two best grades are for: *"Is the existence of virtual studies (MTVU) important within the Megatrend university?"* (9,21) and *"Is MTVU user interface consistent and uniform?"* (9.01).

When it comes to quality, another aspect of Virtual University is extremely important. It is by far the quality of continuous daily maintenance, which results in providing well-functioning MTVU. This task is very complex, demanding, and also alterable due to constant modifications of the courses, program, academic institutions, educational regulations, substantial reforms, and natural fluctuation of academic staff. In addition to this, when one takes into account advances introduced by new ideas, new conceptions and evolution of information technologies, it is clear that daily MTVU maintenance is a complex request.

QUESTIONS	AVERAGE RESULTS
1. How comprehensive are MTVU courses?	**8.15**
2. How substantial are MTVU courses?	**8.26**
3. Are MTVU courses up to date?	**7.89**
4. Grade the balance between theoretical and practical approach in MTVU courses.	**7.42**
5. Are the requirements of the MTVU too high?	**7.89**
6. How do you estimate the quality of knowledge you gain from MTVU?	**7.57**
7. Do you find that the MTVU courses are improving year after year?	**8.05**
8. How do you judge the system of exams grading at MTVU	**8.10**
9. Are professors unbiased and correct at the exams?	**8.31**
10. Are professors precise at the exams grading?	**8.05**
11. Are professors qualified?	**7.94**
12. How difficult are exams on average? (very easy-5, very difficult -10)	**7.89**
13. Is there an improvement of the exams system?	**8.05**
14. Judge the MTVU concept	**8.84**
15. Judge the MTVU implementation	**8.26**
16. Are you satisfied with the MTVU courses' coverage of the curriculum?	**8.05**
17. Are lessons useful in understanding the courses content?	**8.15**
18. Grade the MTVU professor-consultant	**8.26**
19. How much have you been using MTVU virtual professor (not at all -5,… , a lot 10)	**7.94**
20. Are MTVU communication channels useful?	**7.57**
21. Are discussion forums useful?	**7.26**
22. Grade guest lectures in MTVU	**8.21**
23. Are electronic bulletin boards useful?	**8.15**
24. Grade MTVU user interface	**8.94**
25. Is MTVU user interface consistent and uniform?	**9.01**
26. How much MTVU Info helped you in grasping all the MTVU elements?	**7.84**
27. Is the existence of virtual studies (MTVU) important within the Megatrend university?	**9.21**
28. How often have you been visiting MTVU (rearly-5, very often-10)?	**8.68**
AVERAGE OF ALL RESULTS : 8.14	

Table

Maintenance of MTVU is derived from its concept and is proportional to its dimensions. The fact that MTVU contains over 100000 server files, vividly illustrates its size, and consequently the scale of efforts needed for its maintenance – not even to mention MTVU's complexity. MTVU maintenance is divided into the following three main groups:

Maintenance – group A

- Management, control and coordination of MTVU activity
- Communication with the Rector, periodical reports
- Analysis of functions, electronic pools, statistics,...
- Maintenance of MTVU logs of daily events (communications with students, promptness of the reply, individual courses load, enrolment, students logs,....)
- Direct and e-mail communication with students, professors, administrative stuff, publishing sector,..)
- Upload of the new MTVU blocks
- Internet security (defence)
- Internet security (analysis)
- Security backups
- System recovery in the case of eventual system down, reconstruction of complete content and functions
- Participation in marketing and promotions
- Various communication with the "outside world"

Maintenance - group B

- Daily maintenance of each MTVU knowledge base within each of the course-subject
- Maintenance of bulletin boards for each of the institution and each course
- Gathering of all the data necessary for the periodic reports
- Resolving of the daily conflict situations
- Meetings with MTVU students

Maintenance – group C

- Sorting of the daily MTVU information flow into over 60 classes
- Daily responding to the MTVU Info channel:
    - MTVU procedural info

- MTVU academic info
- MTVU technical info

- Daily cooperation with the administrative stuff from the classic Megatrend university
- Daily cooperation with the academic stuff
- Demo presentations for the potential students
- Maintenance of the copy of electronic enrolment data
- Harder considerations and problems

Most of the maintenance tasks are carried out within the MTVU Main Internet Centre.

During the maintenance, along with the main activity, additional new data is generated which should be stored for a period of time. This is done by backing it up in the Main Internet Centre. Incremental backup approach is performed in order to reduce the amount of stored data and, at the same time, to increase the frequency of backup.

Finally, in spite of substantial and complex effort needed to create and maintain Virtual university, this project deserves the strongest support for being a revolutionary learning system and education of the future.

Prof. Dr. Veljko Spasic

7. Globalization of Megatrend University

As repeatedly stressed already, one of the most essential pillars of Megatrend University was to follow the trajectory of globalization. It has embarked on establishment of branch universities in important cities of the world. As Mića Jovanović says, Megatrend University is now in its third phase of development which is a more substantial "internationalization". There are four Megatrend institutions worldwide: International University (Vienna), Institut de Management de Božinoff (Paris), Megatrend Université Chair of Longevity of the Institut De Jaeger (Paris), West London Business School (London) and Teogaku Training School (Tokyo).

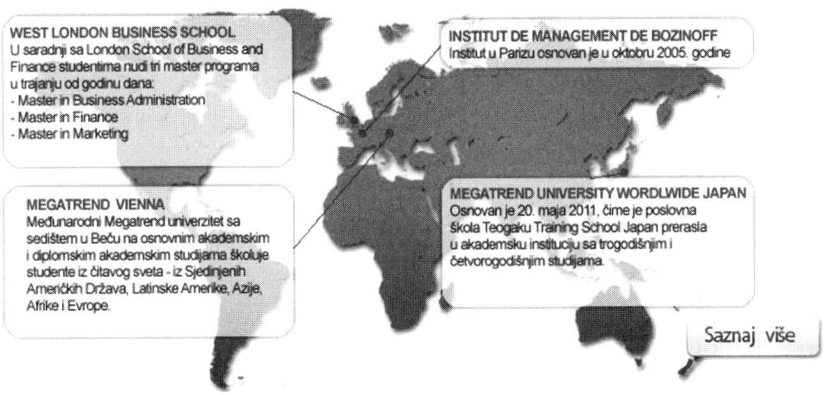

The official start of the newly established International Megatrend University with its headquarters in Vienna took place at the beginning of summer semester in academic year 2011/12. Students from all over the world, mainly from the USA, Latin America, Asia, Africa and Europe study at International Megatrend University in Vienna. There are undergraduate and graduate study programs. The study programs are organized according to the programs and standards of parent Megatrend University in Belgrade and the lectures are conducted in English.

Last, but not least. Megatrend University has been attempting to get a branch campus established in China for some years. For this purpose, the author was assigned to make a feasibility study and contact relevant institutions in Beijing, Shanghai and Nanjing. It looks at the moment that efforts must be continued to bring the already created contact with one of the most famous universities in Beijing to a fruitful result in the near future.

Megatrend Université Paris

Megatrend University in Japan

Megatrend University Worldwide Japan was established on 20th May 2011. The business school Teogaku Training School Japan is an academic institution with three-level and four-level studies. The students from Asia-Pacific region can follow the program of Megatrend University in Belgrade, Vienna and London considering the difficult situation that struck Japan. Teogaku Training School Japan which Megatrend University established in cooperation with Proudfoot Japan, Inc. is based on the Teogaku concept. The concept was created during the rule of imperial family in Japan. It was adapted successfully to Japan's economy which experienced its extraordinary boom.

Dr. Hasegawa, President of Megatrend Teogaku Training School is equipped with abundant experiences and expertise in executive training, especially leadership training in Japan and the USA. Of pivotal importance is that this school is located in the center of the metropolitan Tokyo city, having close connection with the Japanese business world. Advantages Dr. Hasegawa enjoys are as follows: He graduated from the famous Gakushuin University which had tradition to educate princes and princesses of the

Royal Family; the alumni association of this university is extremely strong and Dr. Hasegawa is excellently networked with the business world and consulting companies.

Megatrend University in London

West London Business School, in cooperation with London School of Business and Finance offers three master programs which last for one year:

- Master in Business Administration
- Master in Finance
- Master in Marketing

The three programs can be completed in several ways: studies at campus in London, online studies from Belgrade or the combination of the two studies. Upon completion of the studies, the following degrees are awarded:

- the degree of Megatrend University
- the degree of West London Business School
- the degree of London School of Business and Finance

In cooperation with Grenoble and London School of Business and Finance, there are two programs:

- Bachelor in International Business (for 3 years)
- Master in International Business (for 2 years)

Upon completion of the studies, the following degrees are awarded:

- joint degree of Grenoble and London School of Business and Finance
- the degree of Megatrend University
- the degree of West London Business School

The degree of Megatrend University (the founder of West London Business School in London) is recognized in Serbia and the graduates will not have to validate the degree from London on their return to the country. The students who have completed three-year undergraduate studies can apply for all master studies.

MEGATREND UNIVERSITY IN VIENNA

During internationalization of Megatrend University, a newly established International Megatrend University with its headquarters in Vienna was founded at the beginning of summer semester of academic year 2011/12. Students from all over the world, mainly from the USA, Latin America, Asia, Africa and Europe study at International Megatrend University in Vienna. There are undergraduate and graduate studies. The studies are organized according to the programs and standards of parent Megatrend University in Belgrade, i.e., the Graduate School of Business Studies and the Graduate School of International Economics. The lectures are conducted in English. Active students of the above-mentioned graduate schools are offered the possibility to continue undergraduate and graduate studies at International Megatrend University in Vienna. Megatrend University students and the other students of private and state universities in Serbia have the opportunity to continue their studies in Vienna according to the programs of the Graduate School of Business Studies and the Graduate School of International Economics. The lectures are conducted in English.

Megatrend International University in Vienna

International Megatrend University in Vienna has students from different parts of the world. The University is proud of the fact that there are students from 26 nations, which makes Megatrend University one of few institutions in the country which expand multiculturalism. The work of International Megatrend University in Vienna is carried out under the supervision of the Megatrend University's President Walter Schwimmer, Ph.D., who was Secretary General of the Council of Europe for a number of years, the dean of the Graduate School of Business Studies Ana Milicevic Langovic, Ph.D., and the dean of the Graduate School of International Economics. Branislav Pelevic, Ph.D.

8. National and International Recognitions for Megatrend University

Recent Awards and Acknowledgments for Megatrend University and Prof. Mića Jovanović

The Megatrend University has received many domestic and international rewards and acknowledgements:

- "During 1991, Megatrend Business School, together with the Technical Faculty of Bor carried out the project of introducing management graduate studies. This project, which was the first one of this type in South-East Europe, was financially supported by the European Union TEMPUS Fund which was specifically intended for the development of business education. This success has caused further expanding of Megatrend educational network." (Cited from Wikipedia)
- 2005: The Megatrend University was awarded a Golden Charter of the International Academy of Computer Sciences and Systems, for the loyalty to the initial academic principles and the contribution to the development of applied sciences, and the principal of the Megatrend University. Mića Jovanović, Ph.D., was awarded a Silver Charter for the Vision of the University of Applied Sciences in Modern Times.
- 2006: The principal of Megatrend University Mića Jovanović, Ph.D., was awarded a Golden Ring for the permanent contribution to the culture of Belgrade.
- 2007: In Oxford, a principle of Megatrend University, Mića Jovanović, Ph.D., was awarded the International Socrates Award – given by the Europe Business Assembly – for the strong activity of Megatrend University regarding the plan of improving the international relations in the international recognition of Megatrend University diplomas.
- High acknowledgment Captain Misa Anastasijevic, in the category 2007 Founder, which under the project Road to the Top is awarded by the Republic Chamber of Commerce, Regional Chamber of Commerce Zajecar and Zajecar Municipality, was

awarded to the Megatrend University for the highest achievement in education.

- EDUNIVERSAL –International science committee in Paris, presided by nine eminent professors from the entire world, included the Faculty for Management in Zajecar of the Megatrend University among the top thousand business schools in the world.
- 2008: Chamber of Commerce of Vojvodina and Novi Sad Fair awarded the Megatrend University with the Excellent Design Award. The award was given to the publishing activity of the Megatrend University for the quality of design and publishing culture.
- 2008: Megatrend University was given a Dositej's Charter on behalf of the Pedagogy Movement of Serbia, an acknowledgement established regarding the 200 years of higher learning in Serbia, and the Megatrend University is the only private higher learning institution that received the charter.
- 2008: The Megatrend University was awarded the European Quality Award in the area of education, on behalf of the European Business Assembly.
- 2008: Megatrend University was the first in Serbia to certify the System Quality for the entire University. The certificate for the compliance of the System Quality with ISO 9001:2000 standards was issued by AQA International (American Quality Association).
- 2009: International Science Committee EDUNIVERSAL, within the official selection system, pronounced the High Business School in Zajecar of the Megatrend University among the top five hundred business schools in the world. The EDUNIVERSAL is an organization issuing credits of higher learning institutions all over the world.
- In March 2010, the Megatrend University received a prestigious Vuk Award for the permanent contribution to science, education and culture in Serbia.

Awards and Acknowledgments of Mića Jovanović, Ph.D.

During his long career, Mića Jovanović, Ph.D., received many awards and acknowledgements, domestic and foreign:

- Knight of the British Order of the Fleur de Lys.
- Cultural and educational community of Belgrade awarded in 2002 Mića Jovanović, Ph.D., Golden Badge for the book Intercultural management.
- In 2006 a Golden Ring was awarded for the permanent contribution to Belgrade culture.
- In 2007 an International Socrates Award from the Oxford University was given for the achievement in science, education and culture.
- In 2007 Mića Jovanović, Ph.D., was given an acknowledgement of Grenoble Ecole de Management for extraordinary pedagogical achievement.
- In the organization of European Movement and First European House, Mića Jovanović, Ph.D., was awarded the Best European for 2007 award, for the results in science, culture and education.
- On the ceremony of awarding the international acknowledgements by the European Assembly in Vienna, held on December 8th 2008, Megatrend University and Mića Jovanović, Ph.D., the principle, were given a European Quality Award in the field of education.
- In 2009 Professor Jovanović was elected the expert of the Social and Economic Committee of the European Parliament in Brussels.
- Medal of the Republic of Italy President for significant contribution to European Integrations – high Italian award, given to Mića Jovanović, Ph.D., in May 2009.
- In 2010 Cultural and Educational community of Serbia awarded the Golden Badge to Mića Jovanović, Ph.D., Megatrend University principle, for the contribution to the culture development in Serbia.
- In November 2012, Mića Jovanović was awarded by the Spanish King Juan Carlos I with the highest Spanish decoration for his contribution to the development of civil society.

9. TEMPUS project SIGMUS

In 1991, the great international recognition came from the European Community. Megatrend University was chosen as a partner university for TEMPUS program (SIGMUS).

(The author cites from the internet)

TEMPUS Contract

TEMPUS as European Community's program aims to support higher education in the European Union and Partner Countries focusing on the reform and modernization of higher education systems Eastern Europe, Central Asia, the Western Balkans and the Mediterranean region.

It also aims to promote voluntary convergence of the higher education systems in the Partner Countries with EU developments in the field of higher education. With regards to the Western Balkans, Tempus contributes to preparing the candidate and potential candidate countries for a participation in the integrated Life Long Learning Program.

In addition to promoting cooperation between institutions, Tempus also promotes a people-to-people approach. Tempus provides support to consortia of institutions composed mainly of universities or university associations. Non-academic partners can also be part of a consortium.

The Tempus program is implemented in close coordination with the Erasmus Mundus program which provides scholarships to third country students allowing them to participate in top-level Master courses and Doctorate programs outside the EU.

Background

Since its inception in 1990, university cooperation under the Tempus program has contributed successfully to institution building in higher education in the Partner Countries and to sustainable university partnerships, as well as to enhancing mutual understanding between the academic worlds of the European Union and the Partner Countries.

Particularly in the Partner Countries, higher education institutions are currently facing major challenges linked to (i) dramatic demographic changes (number of people potentially having access to higher education, age structure, migration flows), (ii) increasing global competition, leading to a considerable shift in the distribution of the economic power at world level, (iii) changes in science and technology but notably the growing importance of organizational and societal innovation rather than purely technological innovation and last but not least (iv) challenges of societies in transition (social cohesion, human rights, etc.).

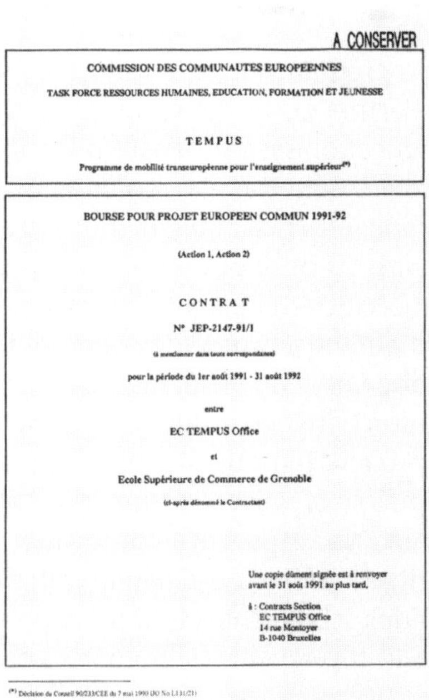

A CONSERVER

COMMISSION DES COMMUNAUTES EUROPEENNES

TASK FORCE RESSOURCES HUMAINES, EDUCATION, FORMATION ET JEUNESSE

TEMPUS

Programme de mobilité transeuropéenne pour l'enseignement supérieur(*)

BOURSE POUR PROJET EUROPEEN COMMUN 1991-92

(Action 1, Action 2)

CONTRAT

N° JEP-2147-91/1

(à mentionner dans toute correspondance)

pour la période du 1er août 1991 - 31 août 1992

entre

EC TEMPUS Office

et

Ecole Supérieure de Commerce de Grenoble

(ci-après dénommé le Contractant)

Une copie dûment signée est à renvoyer avant le 31 août 1991 au plus tard,

à : Contracts Section
EC TEMPUS Office
14 rue Montoyer
B-1040 Bruxelles

(*) Décision du Conseil 90/233/CEE du 7 mai 1990 (JO No L131/21)

Projet Européen Commun TEMPUS — ANNEXE I/1 Conditions spéciales

COMMISSION DES COMMUNAUTES EUROPEENNES
TASK FORCE RESSOURCES HUMAINES,EDUCATION,FORMATION ET JEUNESSE

TEMPUS

Programme de mobilité transeuropéenne pour l'enseignement supérieur(*)

ANNEXE I

PROJET EUROPEEN COMMUN TEMPUS 1991-92

CONDITIONS SPECIALES

Contrat N°: JEP-2147-91/1

Contractant: Ecole Supérieure de Commerce de Grenoble

Organisations participantes:

UNIVERSITY OF BELGRADE IN BOR (YU)
ÉCOLE SUPÉRIEURE DE COMMERCE DE GRENOBLE (F)
ERASMUS UNIVERSITEIT ROTTERDAM (NL)
MEGATREND INTERNATIONAL EXPERT CONSORTIUM LTD (UK)

Titre du PEC: Bor Business School, Bor, Yugoslavia

(*) Décision du Conseil 90/233/CEE du 7 mai 1990 (JO N° L131/21)

Higher education institutions are therefore key players in the successful transition to a knowledge-based economy and society and they provide the training for a new generation of leaders. They are the pools of expertise and centers for the development of human resources. Higher education institutions are also important factors in growth and competitiveness, and play a crucial role in the reform agenda of both EU Member States and the Tempus Partner Countries.

Objectives

The overall objective of Tempus is to contribute to the creation of an area of cooperation in the field of higher education between the European Union and the Tempus Partner Countries.

The specific objectives of Tempus are as follows:

- To promote the reform and modernization of higher education in the Partner Countries;
- To enhance the quality and relevance of higher education to the world of work and society in the Partner Countries;
- To increase the capacity of higher education institutions in the Partner Countries and the EU, in particular their capacity to cooperate internationally and to continually modernize;
- To assist them in opening up to the world of work and the society at large in order to:
  - overcome inter-country fragmentation in the area of higher education and inter-institutional fragmentation in the countries themselves;
  - enhance inter-disciplinary thinking and working within and between faculties and universities and trans-disciplinarity between university faculties;
  - enhance the employability of university graduates;
  - make the European Higher Education Area more visible and attractive to the world;
- To foster the reciprocal development of human resources;
- To enhance mutual understanding between the peoples and cultures of the EU and the Partner Countries.

Priority themes under Tempus are defined around the main components of the EU's higher education modernization agenda and are therefore structured in the following three building blocks:

- **Curricular Reform**
  - Modernization of curricula in academic disciplines identified as priorities by the Partner Countries, using the European Credit Transfer System (ECTS), the three cycle system and the recognition of degrees

- **Governance Reform**
  - University management and services for students
  - Introduction of quality assurance
  - Institutional and financial autonomy and accountability
  - Equal and transparent access to higher education
  - Development of international relations
- **Higher Education and Society**
  - Training of non-university teachers
  - Development of partnerships with enterprises
  - Knowledge triangle education-research-innovation
  - Training courses for public services (ministries, regional/local authorities)
  - Development of lifelong learning in society at large
  - Qualifications frameworks

National and regional priorities are defined based on these themes.

What is European Tempus Project Sigmus?

Sigmus means "Strengthening Student Role in Governance and Management of the Universities of Serbia".

The Project SIGMUS (Strengthening Student Role in Governance and Management of the Universities of Serbia) is designed to strengthen the role of students in governance and management at the Universities of Serbia in line with the Bologna process. The project is one of the National priorities for Structural Measures for Serbia in the area of Governance Reform – University management and student services.

Strengthening of student representative bodies will be made through detailed planning of capacity building of the student representative bodies. Establishment and development of student services at Serbian Universities is another important task of the project. The project results will be disseminated nation-wide, but will be also available to the higher education institutions in the area. Having in mind that the project is of high national priority, it has a full support from all Serbian Universities, as well as from the Ministry of Education and the National Council for Higher Education; this is the best guarantee for sustainability of the project beyond its duration."

Project Background

In the previous years, the higher education reform in the Republic of Serbia was conducted entirely in the spirit of the Bologna Process and encompassed the principal aspects of this Process, including:

- ECTS, curriculum development base on learning outcomes,
- new architecture of Higher Education (three tier system),
- external and internal quality assurance,
- accreditation,
- qualifications frameworks,
- Law on Higher Education (2005).

After the adoption of the Law on Higher Education in 2005, Serbia started a new phase of the HE reform in line with the Bologna declaration and the best practices in EU. However, universities have primarily been focused on reforming curricula and the university governance and management structure. The place, role and responsibility of students in the reform of higher education in Serbia have been recognized, but not yet clearly defined."

National partners:

- University of Belgrade
- University of Novi Sad
- University of Nis
- Ministry of Education
- National Council of Higher Education
- Megatrend University
- Etc.

International Partners:

- Technical University of Crete
- University of Maribor
- University of Udine
- Middlesex University
- Student Union BOKU

10. Publications and Megatrend Review

It is important for the author to list up joint research results and publications with Mića Jovanović. He has been active not only in teaching, but also in joint research and book publishing. It is also important to stress that Megatrend University has been publishing an internationally renowned academic journal 'Megatrend Review'.

Global Cultural and Economic Research:

The joint publication of Mića Jovanović and the author has been continuously carried out in parallel to the birth and development of Megatrend University.

The first joint publication was Mića Jovanović, Sung-Jo Park et al (eds.) 1991: ***Technology and Labor in the Automotive Industry***, Campus Frankfurt/New York.

This book was based on the Proceedings of the Seoul International Symposium sponsored by the Korean Automobile Association (KAMA) containing Jovanović's article "The Business of the Century": The De-Coupling of Business and Self-Management", and Park's article "Prospects of the World Automotive Industry in the 1980s", KAMA/Campus Frankfurt/New York.

The second book was Sung-Jo Park and Mića Jovanović (eds.) 1995: ***What is behind the Japanese Miracle?*** Megatrend International Expert Consortium. This was the Proceedings of the 6th International Conference of the European Association of Japanese Studies, 1991.

Facing the ongoing globalization, both authors, with some other colleagues, came to the idea to deal intensively with intercultural problematiques. The author invited Mića Jovanović to join publication of the Series "Discourses on Intercultural Competence" in 1998 at Free University Berlin, where papers of substantial value for intercultural management problems were published. The scope of the series was described as follows: "(...) Discourses on Intercultural Competence accompanies the genesis of the new global system in exploring the far-reaching implications for structures, strategies and philosophies. In the light of the increasing complexity and discontinuity the series understand globalization as an international socialization-and learning process. (...)"

The scope was more clearly defined as comprising the following fields :

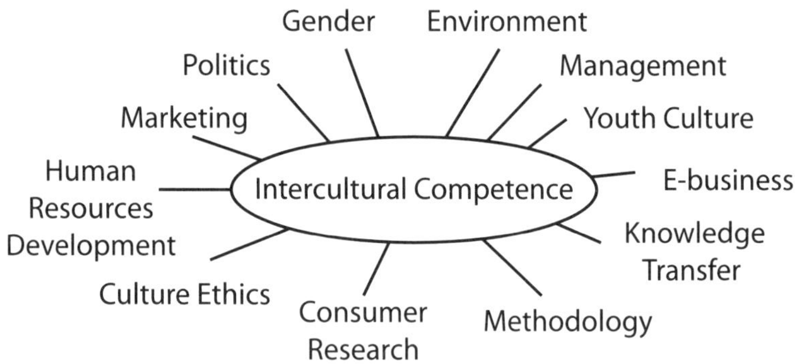

The editorial board was composed of scholars like Profs. Galen Amstutz (Harvard),Tuvia Blumenthal (Ben-Gurion University), Peter Duus (Stanford), Sam Dzever (Nantes), Nitta Michio (Tokyo University), Pan Eng Fong (Singapore Management University), etc.

The series which ceased in the meantime attracted concerned scholarly circles because of the problem-setting and broad spectrum of globalization aspects.

In 2004, Mića Jovanović and the author embarked on the new series with the famous publisher LIT Berlin in 2004 under the title **Global Cultural and Economic Research**

This series has gained an internationally high reputation and published the following publications:

- Sabine Adolph 2006:
  Sumo: Internationalisierung des japanischen Sports
- Sung-Jo Park and Jongwon, Lee (eds.) 2006:
  Economic Cooperation and Integration in Northeast Asia
- Mića Jovanović, Lee Dalgon, Oh Yean-Cheon, Sung-Jo Park and Bernhard Seliger (eds.) 2007:
  System Transformation in Comparative Perspective
- Testsuo Abo (eds.) 2010:
  Competing Chinese and Foreign firms in Swelling Chinese Economy

- Myungkyu Park, Bernhard Seliger and Sung-Jo Park (eds.) 2010:
  Europe - North Korea - Between Humanitarianism and Business?
- Puntsagdash Luvsandor, Chuluundorij Khashchuluum, Namsrai Batnasan (eds.) 2011:
  Mongolia at the Market
- Celal Bayari 2011:
  Japanese Hybrid Factories in Australia
  The Japanese System Transferred
- Celal Bayari 2012:
  Australian Economy and Neo-Liberalism
  Manufacturing, Trade and Bilateral Links with Japan in the Post-Keynesian Age

Megatrend Review - *The International Review of Applied Economics*

This Journal is the periodical of Megatrend University, whose spread stretches over the boundaries of Southeast Europe, Eastern Europe to Asia and USA.

Mića Jovanović writes in the Editorial of Megatrend Review, Vol.7, No.2, 2010 as follows: *"Megatrend Review becomes a place for intensive gathering and interaction of opinions and views on current events in national, regional and international economies with all challenges emerging in the field of global economy, economic policy and development, financial markets and business in present crisis period"*.

This Journal has two goals; the first goal is to reflect on national and regional aspect in the context of globalization; the second one is to focus on Southeast Europe. These two goals are complementing each other and also very plausible for finding proper ways for system transformation in former socialist economies.

Megatrend Review is published semi-annually in Serbian and English. Through the theme approach to the contemporary fields of the social and natural sciences applicable in economics, Megatrend Review reflects the interdisciplinary aspect of the studies at Megatrend University.

Each paper is reviewed by two anonymous reviewers. Articles, which receive positive reviews, are published in accordance with the standard article categorization as original scientific papers, scientific review papers, expert articles, and book reviews. (Cited from the website of Megatrend Review)

The Megatrend Review, even though it is only 6 years old, is internationally known due to high quality of articles, refined management of handling and screening articles and last but not least, specific regional focus. It is registered by the Board of Social Sciences, Ministry of Science, Serbia, and in the International Bibliography of Social Sciences (LSE), and also published in EBSCO's Database "Business Source Complete", and lastly, registered by Leibniz Institute for the Social Sciences.

The following registration is from the Library of Congress Catalogue:

Megatrend Review : The International Review of Applied Economics.

Relevance:	* * * * *
LC control no.:	2007201331
LCCN permalink:	http://lccn.loc.gov/2007201331
Type of material:	Serial (Periodical, Newspaper, etc.)
Uniform title:	Megatrend revija. English.
Main title:	Megatrend Review : The International Review of Applied Economics.
Published/Created:	Belgrade : ill. ; 24 cm.
Description:	v. : Megatrend University of Applied Sciences, [2004]- Year 1, no. 1 ('04)-
ISSN:	1820-4570
Linking ISSN:	1820-4570

11. TV METROPOLIS

(Contribution by Ms. Ljubica Urosevic)

In Serbia, there are many TV stations, state-owned and private. One of the private TV stations is TV Metropolis, unique in the sense that there is an intensive cooperation between Megatrend University and Metropolis TV.

Megatrend University has developed a comprehensive system of integrated educational communication. Since 2001, the Metropolis Television has become an integral part of Megatrend educational system and a teaching basis of Graduate School of Culture and Media. This makes Megatrend University unique, since it is the founder of a TV station which is not of an integral type, but also an official broadcaster, competing with all other TV stations in Serbian media space.

In the open competition of the Republic Broadcasting Agency of Republic of Serbia, the Metropolis TV was officially awarded a regional frequency for broadcasting in 2006. But thanks to the cable broadcasting, the coverage is much wider and the Metropolis TV is watched all over Serbia. The program of the Metropolis TV is broadcast also via satellite, so that it goes beyond regional borders, making the program available to the viewers all over the world. Today, the Metropolis TV is the regional broadcaster of the 24-hour program.

Although it was positioned in the media space as a music television, which attracted a large number of spectators, as it was the only specialized music TV in Serbia, through its further development, the Metropolis TV outgrew its initial music direction. Its program concept has expanded to other fields related to the interests of the young, but also to the needs of the wider range of spectators, offering them the range of attractive TV shows on modern culture, science, technology and phenomena of contemporary society.

The overall program philosophy of the Metropolis TV is dedicated to expansion of growth, motivation for achievement, development of talent and creative initiative, creation of positive life attitudes and promotion of the real values in all fields of life, spreading of tolerance and a cosmopolitan spirit. In short: the creation of a life style characterized by the qualities such as: *successful, open, creative.*

Having in mind the fact that the founder of the TV station is Megatrend University, special attention is dedicated to the program of educational content. Through this program, the public is informed both on higher education in Serbia and on the trends of the university education development in the world. A large number of TV shows covers the life of students and their interests. The most important weekly show among students is 'Gaudeamus' covering numerous activities at Megatrend University, primarily the highly developed international cooperation and the visits of the renowned lecturers from all over the world. It also presents the most successful students, their projects and ideas, social and sport activities. Every event of special importance for the University is recorded by the Metropolis TV and reported on the same day through special time slots called 'Gaudeamus Special'. The lectures of the visiting professors can be seen directly on television („Gaudeamus ex cathedra"), which attracts attention of wider public.

The lectures by and discussions with Profs. Arthur Stockwin (Oxford), Jean-Jacques Chanaron (Grenoble), Galen Amstutz (Harvard), Sung-Jo Park (Berlin), Abo Tetsuo (Tokyo), etc. received a wide acceptance in the Serbian society.

The show 'Be Like Me' is a documentary form, portraying exceptional students, not only according to their grades, but also their special talents and abilities, promoting thus the model of success through their example.

There are also other TV shows aimed at informing students in detail on Megatrend University, while the importance of the Metropolis TV becomes fully recognizable during the enrollment campaigns, when the TV program directly contributes to the interest of the young in Megatrend University, either through specialized shows, or quality and attractive overall TV production.

The students of Graduate School of Culture and Media and Graduate School of Art and Design have a unique opportunity for practical work during their studies by participating in the production of TV program, which is the advantage that no other Serbian graduate school can offer.

This media house turned to the young, which is of modern expression, interactive and urban, nurtures the culture of visual thinking, which also contributes to its popularity among the young population. Recognizing the needs of the young, who build their culture on new communication technologies, and introducing general ethical and civilization values through acceptable modern forms are the goals that this television house strives for. As a television of the modern expression, interactive and urban, it nurtures the culture of visual thinking. Through a clearly defined program concept, the Metropolis TV has managed to recognize and meet the needs of the young, offering them attractive shows on advances of modern culture, science, education and phenomena of modern society.

In the time of commercialization, meeting the needs of the lowest tastes, another feature that makes the Metropolis TV unique is its effort to maximally use the potential of television as the media generating knowledge, offering a large amount of educational and scientific program. Recognizing other needs of the young apart from entertainment, and introducing general ethical and civilization values through acceptable and modern forms are the objectives that this television strives for. It attracts wide audience of all generations through its various production, as well as high-quality co-productions, documentaries and scientific and popular series.

12. Epilogue:

To get rich is glorious.

(Deng Xiaoping)

The path Megatrend University went through for last 23 years has been paved with immeasurable barriers and impediments. But Megatrend University was able to overcome all these hindrances. One could describe these experiences with 'a prelude of venture and creativity'.

The circumstances in which the project Megatrend University was launched were incomparably disastrous. An economy with the persistent tradition of self-management, decrease in productivity, and rampant stagnation could not easily comply with and accept the Western management education system aimed at capitalistic human resources development. There were many counter-forces in public sector, organizations and companies. The Bosnian crisis was not only physically deleterious, but also claimed sacrifice in all respects, further leading to the isolation, where Serbia and Megatrend were caught in. New information and expertise related to modern higher education and globalization scarcely reached Megatrend University.

Despite all these impediments, the concerned people, above all, Mića Jovanović and his friends did not despair and did not cease to push the project Megatrend ahead. Foreign scholars helped him in his adventure and took part in this project. This cooperation was invaluable for the success of Megatrend. Today, among all private universities in Europe, this university is the biggest higher educational institution with detachments in Serbia and branch universities abroad, and noteworthy international networking and cooperation universities abroad. Needless to say, Megatrend is a symbol of success. Yes, Megatrend itself is Megatrend.

How does the future of Megatrend University look like? Mića Jovanović referred to two trajectories: *deepening of education quality and globalization.*

Till now, the Megatrend University has been very successful in expansion in Serbia and abroad. The number of students, schools and branch universities is a clear piece of evidence for this. Further, national and international recognitions are supportive of the reputation of Megatrend. In the future, the task remains, however, how to enhance the quality of teaching, research, and science-industry cooperation compared to other competing universities. To be more precise, the question will be to which extent graduates from Megatrend are absorbed by local and international labor market.

The next trajectory is China. In addition to Megatrend in London, Tokyo, Paris, and Vienna - China (eventually including the region Asia Pacific) will be a great challenge for Megatrend University. Preparations are ongoing. In which form Megatrend is going to launch its project in China will depend again on venturesomeness and creativity.

Bibliography

- Albert, Michel, 1993: *Capitalism against Capitalism, London*
- Florida, Richard, 2002: *The Rise of Creative Class. And how its Transforming works, Leisure and Everyday Life, Basic Books*
- Hall, Peter A. & Soskic, David, 2001: *Varieties of Capitalism, Oxford University Press*
- Jovanović, Mića and Park Sung-Jo, 1995 (eds): *What is behind the Japanese Miracle? London-Berlin-Tokyo*
- Jovanović, Mića, 1980: *Sociology of Self-Management ,Beograde*
- --,1991: 69 Lessons on Management , Beograde
- --, 2002: Works Motivation and Self-Management ,London
- --, 2007: *An Assessment of system transformation in Serbia: the Case of Self-Management Reform, in: System Transformation in Comparative Perspective, Jovanović et al (eds), LIT Berlin, pp 187 ff*
- --, 2008: *Business as Art of Living, Beograde*
- Machlup, Fritz 1962: *The Production and Distribution of Knowledge in the United States*
- Meske, Werner,2004: *Analyzing the Transformation of S&T in CEEEs – the Theoretical and Methodological Approach, in: Meske, Werner (ed), From System Transformation to European Integration, LIT Berlin*
- O'Donnell , Guillermo and Schmitter, Philippe,1986: *Transition from Authoritarian Rule. Tentative Conclusions about Uncertain Democracies, Baltimore/London, Johns Hopkins University Press*
- Oh, Yean-Cheon, 2007: *Human Resources Development for System Transformation: the Case of Asia Development Institute, in: System Transformation in Comparative Perspective, Jovanović et al (eds), LIT Berlin, pp 205 ff.*
- *Radosevic, Slavo 2004: What future for S&T in the CEES in the 21st Century?, in: Meske, op.cit. pp.443 ff.*
- *Seliger, Bernhard 2007: Economic Transformation after 15 years – a Reassessment, in: System Transformation in Comparative Perspective… op.cit., pp. 45 ff*

Appendix I

Additional Institutions that Megatrend has Cooperation with

- West University of Timisoara, Romania
- University of Pec, Hungary
- University for Economics, Bratislava, Slovakia
- Ortega y Gasset, research institute, Madrid, Spain
- St. Ivan Rilski, University for Mining and Geology, Sofia, Bulgaria
- Mediterranean University of Podgorica, Podgorica, Montenegro
- Universidad de Chile, Santiago de Chile
- Universidad El Salvador, Buenos Aires, Argentina
- Russian Academy of Science, Moscow, Russia
- Universidad Simon Bolivar, Caracas, Venezuela
- St Petersburg State University of Service and Economy, St Petersburg, Russia

Appendix II

Mića Jovanović's Interview with Joongang Daily (1997-8-26)

[중앙일보] 입력 1997년 08월 26 "빌딩과 자동차가 무척 많아졌지만 무엇보다 일반 시민들의 모습이 훨씬 멋있어지고 표정이 밝아졌습니다."

세계정치학회 서울대회 참석차 최근 한국을 찾은 미카 요바노비치 (44) 유고슬라비아 메가트렌드경영대 총장은 한국인들의 자신감 넘친 모습에서 깊은 인상을 받았다고 밝혔다.

그는 런돈경제대에서 경제학박사 학위를 받았으며 런던경제대에서도 수학한 동구권 안의 저명한 경영학자다.

메가트렌드경영대는 동구권이 붕괴된 직후인 지난 89년 설립됐으며 현재 3천7백여명의 학생이 재학중이다.

옛 공산권국가를 통틀어 가장 훌륭한 경영대라고 자신의 학교를 소개한 요바노비치 총장은 "역사는 비록 오래 되지 않았지만 자본주의와 시장경제를 배우려는 학생들의 열의만은 정말 대단하다" 고 말했다.

유고 유일의 자동차업체인 자스타바사의 회장 상담역으로도 활동하고 있는 요바노비치 총장은 한국자동차업체와의 협력에도 큰 관심을 표시했다.

이 회사는 한때 연간 20만대 생산에 미국수출까지 했으나 옛 유고연방 해체이후 연간 생산량이 1만대 이하로 줄어드는등 극심한 침체에 빠져 지금은 외국업체 인수만을 기다리고 있는 상황이다.

이때문에 한때 현대자동차의 인수설이 나돌기도 했다.

그는 "한국의 경우 어느나라에도 의존하지 않는 독자적 기반을 가진 자동차산업을 성장시켰다" 며 "한국업체들이 자스타바를 인수한다면 훌륭한 협력모델이 될 수 있을 것" 이라고 기대감을 표시했다.

현재 유고는 보스니아사태와 관련, 세르비아계를 지원하고 있다는 문제로 유엔의 제재를 받고 있다.

이와관련, 요바노비치 총장은 "유엔의 제재속에서도 지난해 유고의 물가상승률은 4.5%에 지나지 않았고 지난 3년동안 안정된 환율을 유지하고 있다" 며 "유고는 옛 공산권국가중 가장 소득수준이 높고 성장 잠재력이 큰 나라" 라고 소개했다.

김원배 기자

기고자 : 김원배

Appendix III:

Tempus project JP 158926–2009 GOVERNANCE AND MANAGEMENT REFORM IN HIGHER EDUCATION IN SERBIA (GOMES)

(we cite a part of Tempus project from the Internet)

Governance and Management – The Structure, Practice, Experience And Challenges in Further Development
The Contribution of Megatrend University, Belgrade

Rector: Prof. Mića Jovanović, Ph.D.

Team:
- Prof. Oskar Kovac, PhD; a member of the National Council for Higher Education
- Radmila Saric
- Gordana Cerovic
- Aneta Marinovic
- Mile Sekulic
- Ljiljana Kojovic
- Aleksandra Zivaljevic
- Jovana Radonjic
- Goran Marjanovic
- Dejan Knezevic

1. Strategic Priorities and Objectives of the University

The main objective of Megatrend University has always been to realize two parallel dimensions of its activity in higher education. On the one hand, its task is to functionally perform and enhance undergraduate, graduate and doctoral studies in the fields of humanities, scientific and mathematical, technical and technological sciences and artistic creation.

The University realizes these parallel main dimensions of educational objectives on the basis of long-term and short-term plans and program documents which are passed by the University Senate and Council, and which are obligatory for all University institutions. On these grounds Megatrend is an integrated university in all its main functions. This is secured by the fact that all statutes and normative acts of departments are subordinate to the similar acts of the University. These are exactly the characteristics of the integrated university, and not the quality or a lack of quality of the legal entity of its parts.

In teaching activities the lecturers are not only mobile and can lecture at other graduates schools of the University, but particular departments, for example Department of Computer Science, organizes computing courses at all other departments, and such useful cross combinations can be found among the schools of social sciences and humanities. Postgraduate and doctoral studies of some schools within the same fields are designed as joint programs. Although Megatrend University schools could have been accredited only separately with the Ministry of science, the whole scientific activity within University has been fully integrated. All the projects are accessible to all lecturers/professors; project teams are selected at the level of university, and not individual schools. The same is true of the widely developed international educational and scientific cooperation of the University. Megatrend University system of quality which secures quality of work in all major activities according to standards ISO 9001.2001 has been awarded a certificate for the University and its schools by the American institution AQA.

The information system which is used at the University and its schools, common services, teaching, scientific work and the library, has been fully integrated. The publishing activity of the University which covers the needs of all schools is also integrated.

Financial operations and investments are planned and carried out on the basis of the University bodies' decisions. The balance sheet of the University involves the schools' operations as well. Investment into space, equipment and lecturers/professors' further education is planned by the University in cooperation with the schools.

In all mentioned fields the policy is created by the University, and the schools apply it creatively and in close mutual cooperation.

The University objectives are determined by the objectives of the schools. Under the circumstances both of these were reviewed thoroughly during the auto-evaluation and while the University was preparing for the accreditation. The following are common for these objectives:

a) continuous innovation of the content and methods of teaching at all three levels of academic studies, as well as vocational studies;
b) provision of high-quality distance learning through the Internet on the basis of multiple educational resources combined in the unique platform (MTVU) in accordance with the demanding requirements and potentials of the field of computer assisted learning, and on the basis of the guided discovery.
c) realization of the joint graduate studies with the renowned foreign universities;
d) increase of students and teachers' mobility in accordance with the newly opened EU programs in particular countries;
e) strengthening scientific production, particularly of younger teachers/lecturers so that they would completely and timely fulfill the promotional criteria;
f) strengthening the cooperation with the economy through establishing a business incubator (with the help of European Investment Bank) on Megatrend University ground near Belgrade airport.

All these objectives, explained through the individuals in charge and their phases of realization, are set out in the annual and mid-term plans of education and other integrated function of the schools and the University. They are harmonized with the mission and main objectives of Megatrend University, and prove its existence and development to be justifiable.

2. A Short Historical Review of the University Development

In the 23rd year since its foundation, Megatrend University has mostly achieved its mission, which started with the cooperation with the highest quality world institutions (the network of Megatrend institutions in the world, Business School in Grenoble and the first Tempus project approved to Serbia). This mission has determined the goals and objectives of the University of today, but also its current capacities and capabilities. Today Megatrend University comprises 12 graduate schools and 3 colleges with more than 26,000 students.

3. Geographical Position of the University

Megatrend University is located in Belgrade, the capital of Serbia, where numerous high schools are, much of Serbian industry, as well as home and foreign trade of Serbia. However, Megatrend University has schools in a large number of Serbian regions.

Starting from the constitutional and civilization norm on the right of everybody to education under the same circumstances, Megatrend University has covered a considerable part of the territory of Serbia with the network of its graduate schools and colleges (Eastern Serbia, Western and Central Serbia and Branicevo, South Banat and North Backa regions). These institutions contribute considerably to the economic, social and cultural development of the mentioned regions of Serbia.

University center for distance learning and its points in the Republic of Serbia make studying possible for those who otherwise could not be able to achieve it.

4. General Data and Numbers on the University

4.1. The Data on the University and its Units: University and a University Unit, Date of Foundation, Location, Legal status, State/Private

1. Megatrend University (20.06.2000).[2]
   Belgrade, Goce Delceva str. 8
   Independent higher education institution
   Legal entity
   Private

2. Graduate School of Business Studies (15.12.1998).
   Belgrade, Goce Delceva str. 8
   Higher education institution
   Legal entity
   Private

3. Graduate School of Management (9.09.1997).
   Zajecar, Park suma Kraljevica
   Higher education institution
   Legal entity
   Private

4. Graduate School of International Economics (14.05.1999).
   Belgrade, Bul. umetnosti 29
   Higher education institution
   Legal entity
   Private

5. Graduate School of Culture and Media (20.09.2005).
   Belgrade, Goce Delceva str. 8
   Higher education institution
   Legal entity
   Private

---

2 Year of accreditation or re-accreditation.

6. Graduate School of State Administration (19.09.2005).
Belgrade, Bul. umetnosti 29
Higher education institution
Legal entity
Private

7. Graduate School of Computer Sciences (9.10.2009).
Belgrade, Bulevar umetnosti 29
Higher education institution
Legal entity
Private

8. Graduate School of Art and Design (21.03.2006).
Belgrade, 29 Bul. umetnosti
Higher education Institution
Legal entity
Private

9. Graduate School of Business Studies (19.09.2005).
Pozarevac, 36 Stari korzo
Higher education institution
Legal entity
Private

10. Graduate School of Business Studies (26.12.2006).
Vrsac, Omladinski trg 17
Higher education institution
Legal entity
Private

11. Graduate School of Business Economics (4.10.2005).
Valjevo, Pop Lukina str. 26
Higher education institution
Legal entity
Private

12. Graduate School of Biofarming (10.03.2006).
    Backa Topola, Marsala Tita str. 39
    Higher education institution
    Legal entity
    Private

13. Megatrend Business College (27.12.1989).
    Beograd, Kralja Petra Str. 46
    Higher education institution
    Legal entity
    Private

14. Management College (16.02.1994).
    Zajecar, Park suma Kraljevica
    Higher education institution
    Legal entity
    Private

15. Institute for New Technologies (10.12.1998).
    Belgrade, Goce Delceva str. 8
    Legal entity
    Private

4.2. Scientific – Research or Educational and Artistic Fields

a) Scientific, i.e. artistic fields
   1. Social sciences and humanities
   2. Natural and mathematical sciences
   3. Technical and technological sciences
   4. Arts

b) Scientific, i.e. artistic fields
   1. Economic sciences
   2. Management and Business
   3. Law
   4. Cultural sciences and communication
   5. Computing
   6. Bio-technical sciences
   7. Applied arts and design, Painting, Drama and Audio-visual arts

Global Cultural and Economic Research
editors-in-chief: Prof. em. Dr. Dr. h.c. Sung-Jo Park (Free University Berlin) and
Prof. Dr. Mica Jovanovic (Megatrend University of Applied Sciences, Belgrade)

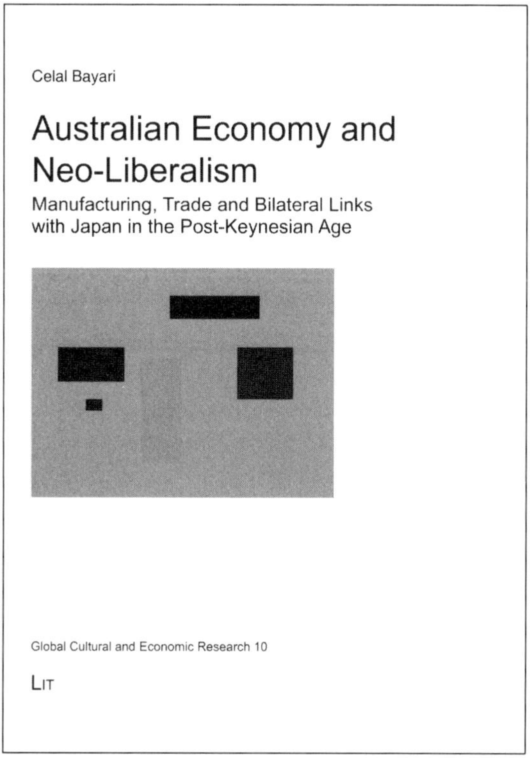

Celal Bayari
Australian Economy and Neo-Liberalism
Manufacturing, Trade and Bilateral Links with Japan in the Post-Keynesian Age
Australian economy has long been typified by neo-liberal governance, foreign investment dependence, exports dominated by grains, resources and energy, and an industrial structure in which foreign multinational enterprises play the leading role. These factors, in combination, have not always contributed to a stable growth and a strong manufacturing sector. Further, they have not always led to the best outcomes for Australia in its integration into the regional and global patterns. These themes form the focus of this book, which presents an analysis of the economic orthodoxy and its effects.
Bd. 10, 2012, 232 S., 29,90 €, br., ISBN 978-3-643-90227-6

LIT Verlag Berlin – Münster – Wien – Zürich – London
Auslieferung Deutschland / Österreich / Schweiz: siehe Impressumsseite

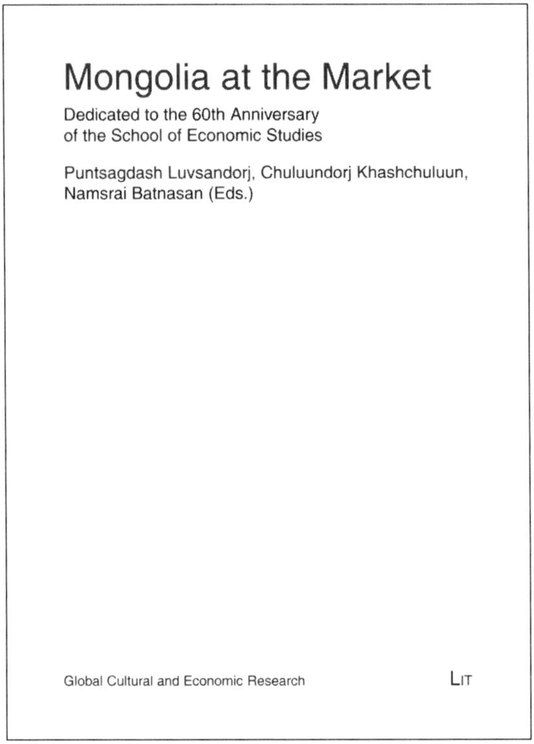

Mongolia at the Market

Dedicated to the 60th Anniversary
of the School of Economic Studies

Puntsagdash Luvsandorj, Chuluundorj Khashchuluun,
Namsrai Batnasan (Eds.)

Global Cultural and Economic Research

LIT

Puntsagdash Luvsandorj; Chuluundorj Khashchuluun; Namsrai Batnasan (Eds.)
Mongolia at the Market
Dedicated to the 60th Anniversary of the School of Economic Studies
"Mongolia at the market" puts forward an aim to study at the national level in a comprehensive way the process of economic transition and development in the years since Mongolia started the transition to market economy; to describe the new market economic system of Mongolia on the basis of analysis of economic branches, sectors, market components; to examine issues of transition and development, which determine trends of national economic development.
Bd. 7, 2012, 496 S., 49,90 €, br., ISBN 978-3-643-90213-9

LIT Verlag Berlin – Münster – Wien – Zürich – London
Auslieferung Deutschland / Österreich / Schweiz: siehe Impressumsseite